# The
# Crisis
# in
# Communism

# The
# Crisis
# in
# Communism:

## The Turning-Point
## of Socialism

**Roger Garaudy**

**Translated
from the French
by Peter and Betty Ross**

Grove Press, Inc., New York

ISBN: 0-394-47587-9 tr.
ISBN: 0-394-17763-0 pb.

Library of Congress Catalog Card Number: 74-155124

Distributed by Random House, Inc., New York

Manufactured in the United States of America by
The Book Press, Brattleboro, Vermont

9 8 7 6 5 4 3 2
First Printing

# Contents

# Acknowledgements

The translators and publisher gratefully acknowledge the help of Mr Maurice Cornforth in the final revision of the translation.

Permission to quote the following material is also gratefully acknowledged: from *The New Industrial State*, copyright © by John Kenneth Galbraith 1967: Hamish Hamilton, London, and Houghton Mifflin, Boston, Mass.; from *Collected Works* of V. I. Lenin, English translation: Lawrence & Wishart, London; from *Selected Works* of K. Marx and F. Engels, English translation, 1950: Lawrence & Wishart, London; from *Works* of J. V. Stalin, English translation: Lawrence & Wishart, London.

# Introduction

It is no longer possible to remain silent.

The international communist movement is in a state of crisis. The Sino-Soviet split, the invasion of Czechoslovakia in 1968, the Moscow Conference in June 1969, the Czechoslovak Party's extorted disavowal of its protests of August 1968, are all clear manifestations of this fact.

Every one of us, in these final decades of the twentieth century, is faced with a fundamental problem. Consciousness of that problem necessarily involves a sense of personal responsibility for its solution, a solution upon which hangs the fate of the world—its agony or its resurrection.

It is a world-wide problem, for it does not concern communists alone; there is no one anywhere who is not involved in its solution.

These reflections are based on particular events in 1968, in the spring of Paris and the spring of Prague, as also upon the trauma resulting from those abortive springs.

First let us take a look at the impasse in French politics and the possible ways of emerging from it.

Among the more curious paradoxes in France today is the fact that, though the Opposition has a majority, it is at the same time impotent.

The victories it achieves are negative victories which in no way contribute to the building of a new future.

In May and June 1968 there was a rising of all the truly live forces in the nation. Nearly ten million employees went on strike; students and intellectuals were massively represented, as were public servants and, after an interval, the peasants. This rising called in question the régime of personal power and of capital of which that régime is the expression.

A few weeks later elections were held and the party which is the embodiment of that system achieved a considerable victory.

In 1969 there was a referendum. A majority of 'Noes' forced General de Gaulle out of office. Yet a month later his immediate heir was elected president of the Republic.

A similar paradox is found within the Opposition itself. The Communist Party is in the majority and at the same time it is impotent. On two occasions, in the legislative elections of 1968 and the presidential elections of 1969, it won individual victories; it was the only oppositional party which, instead of disintegrating, actually succeeded in consolidating its position.

But like a stronghold in the desert, it finds itself isolated, without any extraneous organized force, without an ally.

This twofold paradox surely calls for investigation.

Now who could be in a better position to take the initiative required to emerge from the impasse—thus rescuing not only the Opposition, but the country itself—and who could better open up prospects for the future than the main organized force in that majority Opposition, the Communist Party, firmly rooted as it is in the working class whose confidence it enjoys because of its mission, which is to embody the revolutionary plan?

I shall end this inquiry with an attempt to answer that question, basing my answer on two convictions which I have come increasingly to regard as truisms:

Nothing valid can be done in France without the Communist Party;

Nothing at all can be done unless that Party radically transforms itself.

The problem posed by the impasse in which the revolution finds itself in France is only a particular case of a more general problem. Although the revolutionary forces in many parts of the world were less numerous a few years ago than they are today, the Communist Parties were the essential magnetic poles within them. Now that those forces have increased they are evincing a strong tendency to 'bypass' the Communist Parties, to evolve outside them, without them, and sometimes in opposition to them.

In Latin America only one socialist revolution has so far been successful—the Cuban—and there the Communist Party, strong though it was, did not initiate the event; it rallied to it. Elsewhere in the continent, under the almost colonial yoke of the most powerful imperialism in the world, there is an explosive situation in which great social forces are awakening to the need for revolution. Of those forces the Communist Parties form only a component part and not always the most dynamic.

In black Africa, where national, anti-colonialist movements are locked in strife with neo-colonialism and its power, wealth and cunning, Marxist Parties are virtually non-existent. In the Moslem world, too, the nationalist, indeed socialist, movement is 'bypassing' the Communist Parties.

In Asia these problems are assuming a particularly dramatic form, not only because of the voluntarist position adopted by the Chinese Communist Party and its aspirations to world hegemony in the movement, but also because of the extermination of the Indonesian Communist Party and internal schisms within the other Parties, notably those of Japan and India. The highest affirmation of the movement's dynamism is being given by the communists in Vietnam who, at the cost of incalculable sacrifices, are victoriously holding their own against the strongest imperial power in the world.

In the developed countries of Europe and America can it really be hoped that, outside of the Communist Parties of France, Italy and Spain, the mass of the working class as well as other revolutionary potential could be won over by the Communist Parties at present in existence?

Hence we must be on our guard against the 'triumphalism' which inspires so many of the passages in the 'Document' put out by the Moscow Conference and must seek to tackle the real problems, not only by recognizing and analysing the basic causes of the contradictions that exist between the socialist countries, but also by trying to discover why so many revolutionary forces are 'bypassing' the Communist Parties.

From now on, drastic 'rethinking' will be necessary—for communists, non-communists and anti-communists alike.

For if the problem is to be posed at all, it must be posed in its entirety. The assertion that human possibilities have increased more during the past twenty years than in the course of several millennia is little more than a cliché.

What has been done in the capitalist countries, even by the richest of them, to adapt human relations to this tremendous mutation?

What has been done in the socialist countries confronted by the same question?

A decisive stage has now been reached as a result of the conquest of three 'infinites':

On the plane of the infinitely small, the harnessing of atomic energy heralds the era of the controlled disintegration of matter, opening up vistas of illimitable wealth and power for man.

On the plane of the infinitely great, the first explorations in space have provided us with an unending prospect of possible transformations and even of human migration into the cosmos: we have crossed the planetary frontiers of space.

On the plane of the infinitely complex, the cybernetic

revolution, namely the introduction of computers, of auto-mated production and of data processing, has, within the space of a few years, supplemented human calculations to such good purpose that man's brain, freed for its creative function, finds its scope suddenly enlarged—so much so, indeed, that his real powers are temporarily outstripping his imagination grown dizzy with the prospects opening out before it.

Thus, while everything seems possible, we cannot but be painfully aware of the gap between our life as it could be and our life as it is. Atomic energy is used in the main to create means of destruction rather than means of pro-duction. The wonderful epic of space research has been turned into a pawn in the game of prestige (with military implications) between the Great Powers. As for the ulti-mate role to be played by cybernetics in human life, noth-ing definite can as yet be predicted. Will it bring about renewed alienation in a technocratic form of totalitarian-ism, or an unprecedented liberation of the creative poten-tial in man, in each and every human being?

Posing the problem in this way does not mean that we are reverting to some form of technological determinism, that we are abandoning ourselves to the evolutionary mechanism of the productive forces alone, whence all forms of social life, from political structures to ideologies, must derive.

We do not hold that, by the mere play of historical en-tropy, the present world will necessarily attain equilibrium, that the United States Government will become socialized by sheer force of circumstances or that, by the same token, the government of the U.S.S.R. will become liberalized.

We do not believe in that primacy of technology and of the productive forces upon which all reformism is based, nor do we believe in the automatic realization of a future whose history is written in advance and not made by men themselves.

Several futures are possible and each one of us is responsible for their actualization. Hence our working hypothesis is far from being a mere technocratic variation of traditional reformism.

It is concerned rather with counteracting the failure to analyse what is fundamental, namely the nature and consequences of the new scientific and technological revolution—a failure characteristic of the Moscow Conference document whereby the communist movement is threatened with impotence—and to do so by restoring to the productive forces the role attributed to them by Karl Marx:

This would be a development of the productive forces such as would give rise to fresh contradictions; in other words, new class relations and new antagonisms which in turn would demand revolutionary forces and a fresh analysis upon which to base their new strategy.

As against somnambulists of whatever persuasion, lost in their dreams of yesterday, we seek in this book to ask three questions:

What *mutations* are at present taking place and to what new contradictions are they giving rise?

What *initiatives* are necessary in order to adapt human relations generally to that mutation?

*Who* will become conscious of the new contradictions and who will take the initiatives needed to resolve them?

There are two further points I shall have to make if I am to elucidate the spirit in which I have tackled these problems.

In this book no concessions are made when criticizing the behaviour of existing Soviet leaders. This is not to imply anti-Sovietism.

To maintain that Lenin's successors, from Stalin to Brezhnev, have, in the eyes of the world, tarnished the splendid image of the October Revolution, to say that their dogmatism has impoverished and disfigured Marxism and has formed an obstacle to a scientific analysis of the contradictions inherent in capitalism, thus restricting the Communist Parties' revolutionary opportunities, to say that, by their conduct—from the excommunication and boycott of Yugoslavia in 1948 to the invasion of Czechoslovakia in 1968—these men have split the movement by effectively refusing to recognize the right to search for socialist models in keeping with the requirements of every nation and every epoch and have, moreover, fettered the building of socialism even inside the Soviet Union—to say all this is not to cast doubt on the significance of the October Revolution, any more than our criticism of the present leaders in Peking casts doubt on the historical significance of the Long March and the Chinese Revolution.

It is as a militant communist and in the certainty that socialism alone is capable of creating social relations commensurate with the exigencies of the tremendous mutation wrought by science and technology, and of exploiting that change in the service of the freedom of all men without exception—it is because of these two factors that I say unequivocally to the Soviet leaders: 'The socialism we want to build in France is not the socialism you are forcing upon Czechoslovakia!'

Needless to say, a man does not have to be a communist to know that anti-Sovietism is a crime against France and against peace. Even those with reactionary political views have understood as much.

Quite independently of any ideological consideration, the Soviet Union's interests of state in the field of international relations would incline her as a rule in the direction of peace. The U.S.S.R. represents a most important counterweight to the imperialist operations of the United States. From Vietnam to Cuba, her economic and military aid forms an efficient bulwark against American world hegemony. In this way she serves the cause of peace and of the national independence of the peoples. The same thing applies to the German problem where the Soviet Union holds in check all attempts to restore neo-Nazi imperialism.

That is why criticism of the present Soviet leaders cannot be extended to the Soviet Union as such without endangering national independence and world peace.

The second point I have to make concerns my own relations with the French Communist Party. Here again self-criticism (and I say 'self-criticism' because I have belonged to the Party executive for more than twenty years and hence must regard myself as partly responsible for its policy), self-criticism of some of its attitudes and analyses does not mean an attempt to undermine it but rather to create the conditions under which it might one day be able to play its role to the full.

The reason why I now find myself obliged to conduct this argument in public is because, for over three years, not one of my suggestions has ever been allowed to break through the barrier of silence which surrounds the proceedings of the Politburo and the Central Committee. Throughout those years I have been constantly told: 'You are absolutely free to say what you think, provided it stays "inside the Party".' But this in itself is a fraud, for the Party is not just the Politburo and the Central Committee; it is the whole body of militants. But, whether out of mistrust or contempt, the opinion of the 'substructure' is never sought. For the substructure is regarded as immature, as incapable of separating the wheat from the tares. Not one of the Party organs, neither *L'Humanité*, nor *France nouvelle*, nor *Cahiers du communisme*, provides its readers with opinions which differ in any respect from the 'official line' of the apparatus.

It is that which has impelled me to write this book and to bring the debate out into the open, both inside the Party and outside it, for it deals with the problems upon which hangs the future both of the Party and of the nation.

Between militants who share the same basic aim—socialism—it should be possible, as each problem arises, to hold open discussions about the best way of solving that problem in order to achieve the common goal and to rally in a common endeavour millions of Frenchmen who, with varying degrees of consciousness and resolution, are pursuing the same goal.

It is no longer possible to remain silent.

This work is not intended to be polemical. What it proposes is common deliberation on the immense initiative required to meet the fundamental mutation of this era, at the same time putting forward working hypotheses on five vital questions:

1. What is the nature of the new scientific and technological revolution? What are its consequences? Are its demands compatible with the development of democracy and with man's creative development?

2. What new contradictions will this mutation bring about in the capitalist countries, more especially in the richest and most powerful of them all, the United States? What steps are being or might be taken to resolve those contradictions?

3. What are the contradictions arising out of the mutation in the socialist countries, and what historical initiatives are being taken to overcome them? Is this demand met by the Soviet model? By the Chinese model? By the Yugoslav model?

4. What profound transformations does that mutation require today
   in the French Communist Party,
   in the Opposition,
   in French policy generally?

5. How will international relations be affected by this mutation? And what steps would make possible, as things are now, a world-wide reorganization of requirements, resources and hopes, that would ensure the full flowering of all men without exception?

Let anyone who will, take up the challenge of this debate. It is no longer possible to remain silent.

# 1 What is the New Scientific and Technological Revolution?

The superficial impression gained from the spectacle of the second half of the twentieth century is one of chaos; conflicts rage from north to south and from east to west, there are savage revolts, ostensibly destructive and no more, and false orders which are not directed towards any particular end.

Do these convulsions, deeper by far than those that marked the end of the world of Antiquity, herald the Apocalypse and the nuclear destruction of the human race? Perhaps.

But to anyone who goes beyond the mere spectacle, the superficial impression, who searches for some kind of unity and meaning, this second half of the twentieth century will appear as something more than a melting-pot of obtuse millenial hopes or of outmoded Utopias. For might not this total crisis prove to be a positive sign, presaging the most radical change in man since the discovery of implements and of fire? Indeed, it might even be a Renaissance beside which that of the sixteenth century would appear provincial and derisory—not a rebirth but in fact the birth of human kind. What, then, is in process of being born? And what must we do to help it achieve fullness of being? For this is something within our capability.

We would like to examine these questions in the light of the events of the past two years, and more especially of four events whose deep significance we believe to be not unrelated. These are:

the student movement,
labour strikes,
the cadres' strong participation in those strikes,

the new political course taken by Czechoslovakia between January and August 1968.

Of all these movements, the one most indicative of a new situation is the student movement which is, of course, linked to that of the cadres.[1] All those involved are confronted by the same problem—their assimilation into the apparatus of production, an assimilation immediately affecting the technologists, engineers and cadres but which for the students is still of the future.

The universality of the student revolt compels us to consider the full extent of this problem, which is also the problem of the cadres. It goes without saying that the universality and, on occasion, even the simultaneity of the student movements should not blind us to their considerable diversity, a diversity that is due to their many different places of origin, whether a country of the third world, a developed capitalist country, or a socialist country. In countries recently freed from oppression the student movement prolongs the nationalist movement and takes a stand against neo-colonialism. In a developed capitalist country the main target is the very principle of a consumer society and the authoritarian régime that often goes with it. In a socialist country the movement may, at one and the same time, call in question the tendency towards a society which might ultimately resemble a capitalist consumer society, while it may also rebel against the bureaucratic forms of the State. There is, however, always the risk that such movements could be exploited, not for revolutionary but for reactionary purposes, by those forces which tend towards maintaining a state of established disorder.

1. It is a *rapprochement* that should not disguise the differences: whereas in the cadres the preoccupation with efficiency and competition plays a major role, the student revolt, with its thirst for absolutes, often shows signs of rejecting these contingencies which are regarded as irrelevant.

There is yet a further factor that cannot be excluded, the so-called phenomenon of resonance, whereby vast numbers of students are carried away by currents which cut across national boundaries, since the problems at issue are not themselves confined within national limits. As examples we might cite the universal struggle against the war in Vietnam, numerous symptoms of contagion by China's cultural revolution, the exaltation of certain models of revolutionary conduct like that of Che Guevara, or again the fascination exercised by some ideologies, such as the philosophy of Marcuse.

But we should not allow all this to blind us to what is essential, to the underlying causes of this general movement which has gripped the student masses and which is increasingly confronting the cadres with fundamental questions.

The very fact that the students' movements should have taken on an extreme form in both capitalist and socialist countries shows that the revolt is not merely concerned with existing productive relations—though there is no denying the importance of this struggle; it also shows that all these movements have a common denominator which should be sought in the development of the productive forces.

The basis of this problem—the common source of these apparently separate movements—seems to me to be this: at a certain stage in the development of the productive forces (that of the present scientific and technological revolution) the full development of man becomes the necessary precondition for historical development if this is not to be held back.

Among students, cadres and workers alike, in France as in Czechoslovakia and the United States, what is forcibly emerging in opposition to the blind mechanisms of industrial civilization, is human *subjectivity* in this, the era of the scientific and technological revolution.

The common denominator of the claims of labour, of the cadres' questioning, of the students' aspirations is a demand for participation, as opposed to alienation from existing structures—participation in historical initiative, in the decisions upon which their fate depends in the sphere of economics, politics and culture. The underlying principle of all the movements in 1968 and 1969 is the refusal to be integrated into a system without being able to discuss its meaning, value or purpose.

The new powers acquired by man in this final part of the twentieth century are not simply an extension of the old ones. In the spring of 1968, in Paris as in Prague, we can detect premonitions of extraordinary growing pains, preceding a qualitative change in human destiny. We stand on the threshold: the new powers man has acquired over himself and over his environment can change his nature as profoundly as did, tens of thousands of years ago, the first discovery of tools.

This technological upheaval is still in its early stages. It seems highly probable that it will give rise in the near future to a permanent revolution in our living conditions as a whole. This, the last part of the twentieth century, may be the epoch of increasing divergencies and of terrible tensions, or again it may be the epoch during which we shall find ourselves able to surmount them. Shall we be capable of mastering the progress of technology, or shall we succumb to it and to anarchy?

Our optimism has an objective historical foundation.

Here I should like to give my own version of a famous axiom: 'A little technology removes us from man and a lot of technology can lead us back to him.' If the technology of the industrial era as it existed in the nineteenth and the first half of the twentieth century had a tendency to crush human subjectivity, the technology of the last part of the twentieth century, that of computerization, can create conditions for an explosion of human subjectivity. And this will be so as soon as it becomes evident that, as from a certain technological level, human investment is the most profitable of all investments—quite aside from all moral, religious or humane considerations and regarded strictly from the point of view of productivity and profitability, not forgetting the problems of the allocation of resources.

## 1. *The Mutation*

In order to broach this problem it is necessary to become conscious of the fundamental mutation now taking place.

1. A revolution *in* science has paved the way for a revolution *by* science.

The mutation that is taking place now is the result of the accumulated discoveries at the level of basic research made since the beginning of this century in the fields of nuclear physics, of macromolecular chemistry, of cybernetics, biology and sociology.

We are witnessing a transformation of science itself: cybernetics has superseded mechanics as the pioneering branch of science.

We are witnessing a transformation of the concept of science. A new subject-object dialectic is emerging; contrary to all empiricism and all positivism, it would seem that the objective world cannot be defined without the man who places himself before that objective reality along with his hypotheses and models.

A scientific fact is always an answer to a question and the answer is always, to a greater or lesser extent, a function of the question that has been asked.

2. The revolution *by* science becomes manifest when the

impact of that revolution *in* science makes itself felt in the technological apparatus of production.

a) *That revolution finds its expression in the ever greater role played by science in production.* The fact that science, in the final part of the twentieth century, is coming more and more to be an immediate productive force is proved by the diminishing time-lag between a scientific discovery and its practical application, its utilization in industry.

A hundred and two years went by before the discoveries which made photography possible were put to practical and industrial use (1727-1829). For the telephone the time-lag was only fifty-six years (1820-1876); for the radio a mere thirty-five years (1876-1902), fourteen for television (1922-1936), six for the atomic bomb (1939-1945), five for the transistor (1948-1953) and five for the laser (1956-1961).

The first consequence of the ever growing role of science as an immediate productive force was the increased importance of brain work in the field of production as a whole.

The spectacular rise in the number of cadres and students is an indication of this. Statistics based upon sixty-two countries show that between 1955 and 1964 the student population rose from seven and a half million to twenty million; in other words, it has just about trebled.

In the United States generally the ratio of engineers to other workers is 10 per cent. In aeronautics it is 13 per cent, in the petroleum industry 20.5 per cent, in the atomic industry 34.1 per cent. The phenomenon we are witnessing here is analogous to the one that took place during the industrial revolution when industrialization quickly inverted the numerical ratio of agricultural to industrial workers. Today we are beginning to perceive a similar inversion in the numerical ratio of manual to intellectual workers.

b) *The revolution also finds expression in a further inversion: the inversion of the relations between science and technology.*

Although this field lends itself no better than any other to one-way mechanistically pre-determined relations between science and technology, and though there is always cross-fertilization and a dialectical relation between technology and science, a new phenomenon has made its appearance, a change of emphasis.

Up till the middle of the twentieth century the demands of technology and production were generally the chief motivational factor in scientific progress. A classic example is the discovery of the highly abstract laws of thermodynamics at the beginning of the nineteenth century (the Carnot, Joule and Mayer principle), which resulted from research by engineers on the maximum performance of steam engines.

Beyond a certain point this relation would appear to become inverted. Scientific progress becomes a motivational factor in the development of production which it precedes and leads on instead of following. Einstein's theories anticipate the utilization of nuclear energy and the deployment of atomic technology. Cybernetics saw the light of day before computers came into use.

To an ever greater extent science is forging ahead independently of the motive force constituted by the demands of production. This seems to presage a new historical law: the more advanced a country both economically and technologically, the more directly will its economic and social progress depend on that of science.

In the United States, expenditure on research exceeds all other forms of investment (twenty thousand million dollars).

And in the United States as in the U.S.S.R. the number of research workers doubles every seven or eight years.

c) *The revolution finds expression in the transformation*

*that has taken place in the very idea of technology*: Just as in science, and correlative with the fact that electronics play an increasingly important part in relation to mechanics, the key to the changes from a technological point of view would appear to be, as McLuhan has suggested, that *communication* in the widest sense of the term—as an extension, that is, of the human body and senses—is taking the place of labour[2] as the basis of the technological system.

This, then, is the great inversion: the cybernetic principle is superseding the mechanical principle. The two most immediate consequences are as follows:

1. *Industrialization* led to a subdivision and to an ever more detailed analysis of work; the new scientific and technological revolution reverses the trend of the industrial revolution, tending not only towards *analysis* but also towards *synthesis*.

2. A second inversion results from the first—the inversion of the relations between subject and object. Whereas by its nature industrial production tended to ignore the subjectivity of the worker—the man, restricted to serving a piece of machinery, became an object subservient to the object (the machine) of which he was an appendage—the computerization of production as also of administration tends to place man at the periphery of direct production, his role being now:

> above the machine, for analysis and programming,
> beneath the machine, to decide and orientate,
> on a level with the machine, to control, by combining the

2. The word 'labour' is used here in the narrowest and crudest sense to mean a man's muscular strength applied to an action upon things. McLuhan uses a paradox to emphasize the fact that knowledge is playing an ever greater role in the very idea of work.

functions of adjuster, maintenance worker and repairer, thus fulfilling the demand for a synthetic, overall view of the whole technological process (even though it may remain a partial one since it will be limited by specialization). This also entails:

an aptitude for posing problems,

frequent refresher courses in view of the rapid development of technological methods.

3. This revolution *in* science and the revolution *by* science which derives from it have given rise to a number of consequences, these being in the first place economic. And here we must avoid two fallacies.

Firstly, the belief that we are witnessing an abrupt and immediate break. In fact there is a very large number of disparate technological levels and social régimes, while in all the economically advanced countries the aftermath of the industrial revolution, which determines the essential character of existence, continues to persist alongside the consequences of the new technological and scientific revolution whose ferment is beginning to affect every aspect of life.

The second fallacy consists in the belief that this mutation will be no more than a passive reflection of changes in the substructure. In fact we shall have to confront a number of possible alternatives, if not a whole new range of possibilities. Hence any form of mechanistic determinism is ruled out; the choices men make, their actions and their struggles will see to that. In considering the economic consequences of the great mutation we can do no more than formulate laws that express a tendency.

*With these reservations, what are the economic consequences of the mutation?*

*a*) First, the formation of a new model of growth.

The new factors in growth are now: technological innovation and education (though both of these remain subordinate to the demands of competition). Up till now economic growth has been chiefly dependent on the accumulation of capital and an increase in the number of active workers. From now on it will depend increasingly on the level attained by scientific research, on a rapid expansion of systems that are completely computerized, and on the human quality of the workers who think out, control and plan production and its administration.[3]

In other words, the *qualitative, intensive* factors in development (application of science, overhaul of techniques, raising of skills, rationalization of administration) will take precedence over *quantitative, extensive* factors (acquisition of more machinery and greater numbers of workers).

*b*) With regard to employment, the consequences seem at first sight alarming:

1. From a quantitative point of view it might be expected that the rapid spread of automation would make large numbers of workers redundant, thus giving rise to a serious unemployment crisis.

But these fears are not borne out by the facts.

In the United States, where automation has developed very rapidly[4] and where there has been a marked increase in population (eight million a year), unemployment figures ever since 1961 have steadily declined: 6.7 per cent in 1961, 5.2 per cent in 1964, 4.7 per cent in 1965, 4 per

3. These remarks should be considered in the light of the limits imposed on this general tendency by the problems of the allocation of resources: a researcher in the field of high energy physics, for example, costs 500,000 francs a year (50 million old francs).

4. The rate, however, is relative: In the United States automation is used only up to about 10 per cent of its potential, in Europe only up to 1 per cent (European Conference on Automation, O.E.C.D., February 1966).

cent in 1966, and a predicted 3.5 per cent for 1968. The evidence goes to show that employment figures will continue to rise until 1975. There is a growing number of vacancies for skilled personnel, the number of unskilled workers remaining more or less stationary.

In other words, as things are now automation is more likely to result in the redeployment of labour than in its elimination. Thus in the long run, and always provided that social relations are harmoniously adjusted to the productive forces, it may be predicted that automation will make possible a shorter working day and considerably more leisure.

2. Does automation result in raising the number of skilled workers or does it reduce many to the status of unskilled labourers? Here again, although from a short-term point of view the latter might have seemed the more probable alternative, this has proved not to be the case.

The general trend, up to the middle of the twentieth century—and persisting in France until round about 1955-56—was towards a lower status, since the percentage of unskilled workers continued to rise.

During the past fifteen years this trend has been in process of inversion.

It should be added that the whole notion of occupational skills has undergone a change. Especially in advanced sectors such as electronics or petrochemistry, skills cannot be acquired once and for all after entering industry by way of a specialized apprenticeship. Increasing automation, both in production and in management, demands an aptitude for grasping the whole of the technological process in order to be able to decipher its messages, while rapid changes in the productive forces require an aptitude for absorbing new technical ideas at frequent intervals if not continuously.

Thus a new and unprecedented phenomenon is the increasingly important part which a certain form of general education is coming to play in occupational skills.[5] American, Czech and Soviet estimates agree in suggesting that twenty years from now, in societies with developed economies, about seventy per cent of all workers, at the time they enter industry, will have to have a general education up to the standard of what is now required for entry into a college of technology.

*c*) The new scientific and technological revolution demands new forms of management.

What appeared most profitable half a century ago, in the heyday of the engineer F. W. Taylor's theory of the rationalization of labour, was maximum concentration of initiative and decision. Here again the new scientific and technological revolution is bringing about a total inversion: from now on what is most profitable is a complex system of centres of initiative and decision (implying a massive increase in the number of technical and administrative cadres while taking into account the employment curve already alluded to).

In this field the great change manifests itself in the transition, in managerial methods, from a rationale of a mechanistic type to a rationale of a cybernetic type.

The rationale of the mechanistic type, both in management and in production, found its most complete expression in Taylor's 'rationalization'. It was characterized by a manipulation of men regarded as things—by depriving them, that is, of their subjectivity. Taylor boasted of having replied, when some of his workers came to suggest certain modifications in the way their work was organized, that since thought slowed down the reflexes, they must re-

5. 'Education', says Kant in his *Critique of Judgement*, 'is the creation in a rational being of an aptitude for any kind of general end.' We still have a long way to go.

frain from thinking, leaving it to those who were paid to do so. This administrative model derives from the concept of an objective rationale of the mechanistic and determinist type, postulating one source of impetus only, from which direct decisions and commands are transmitted through a series of passive cogs in accordance with a strict hierarchy; in an extreme case one man thinks and decides for all the rest.

Now we have seen how, in the field of production, the new scientific and technological revolution demands an ever greater aptitude for synthesis, for posing problems, and for the absorption of new ideas, all of which imply active rather than passive participation in decision-making. This means that it is no longer technically possible to ignore the subjectivity of employees. On the contrary, the subjectivity peculiar to employees becomes an essential factor in development.

The new rationale in management must necessarily integrate this variable: thus the earlier rationale of a mechanistic type must be superseded by a rationale of a new cybernetic kind, comprising the moment of 'feed-back', of retroaction made up of a plurality of centres of initiative including even the smallest administrative cadre. Thereafter management would consist, not so much in issuing and enforcing rigid instructions, as in coordinating and orienting a whole mobile complex of creative centres, all to some extent autonomous and in a state of constant interaction.

It might seem at this point that the computer could oppose that tendency since it makes possible the extreme centralization of information—and hence of decision. On the other hand it also permits the dissemination of information which, in principle, could be available to everyone; in other words, everyone would be in a position to take initiatives and to make decisions autonomously.

The computer demands a non-Taylorian system.

*d*) The growing importance of leisure time is making possible the development of subjectivity, not only *in* work, but *outside* it.

At the industrialization stage the workman's rest period was the time biologically required for the conservation or, at the very best, for the reproduction of labour power. At that stage free time was not independent of work but was its minimal precondition. Hence it could not serve to develop the personality. Leisure of this kind is necessarily passive instead of being active and creative.

The leisure required to meet the demands of the scientific and technological revolution is of a quite different order.

According to Jean Fourastié's estimates (in *Les 40,000 heures*) which approximate very closely to Soviet predictions, at least thirty leisure hours per week would be necessary, assuming a working week of thirty hours and forty working weeks per year.

It is a striking inversion. For the first time in human history everyone would have more free time than working time.

The change would not only be quantitative; in as much as leisure time would exceed working time, it would also be qualitative. Hitherto leisure has played only a minor role—that of making good the wear and tear resulting from work, or of compensating and distracting—a mere precarious respite from the daily round of toil. Its main object has been 'recuperation', a careful husbanding of strength; hence the passive, spectator outlook, the amateur, do-it-yourself activity as a substitute for the creative life, or again the illusory compensation on the periphery of real life provided by the football match, the regular Saturday night visit to the cinema, or the worship of a pop star.

Consumption, whether material or mental, whether of gadgets or comic strips, of sporting papers or films devoted to the plushy adventures of 'idols', reflects and redoubles alienation from production.

A new problem will be posed, not only when free time is in excess of working time, but also when, man's work having brought into play his creative activity, the purpose of leisure is no longer his recuperation from exhaustion but the furthering of his creativity and the definition of his aims. This already applies to the artist or the research worker for whom there is no sharp dividing line between leisure and work.

What will leisure become when human ends are no longer circumscribed by dotted lines, or foredoomed to meaninglessness through the sheer necessity of overcoming penury? What will leisure become when work is no longer a ransom exacted for the satisfaction of needs? What will leisure become when morality is no longer, as in the world of penury and abnegation, the observance of rules but the creation of rules, when aesthetics takes the place of ethics, when the burning problems of the day will be Jean Rostand's questions: 'In what image will man seek to recreate himself? Where can the craft of God be learnt?'

*e*) The great inversion, which is found in the first instance at the level of work, is fundamentally an inversion of the relations between subject and object.

Industrialization in the age of simple mechanization, the age of 'mechanism', inevitably led to the fragmentation of labour, breaking it down into the elementary gestures demanded by the machines. It also led to the transformation of man, as Marx has it, into a 'mere living appendage in a lifeless mechanism', no more than a stopgap in the process of mechanization in as much as his presence, *qua* link in the transmission of power, was less costly than that of a machine.

This 'division of labour', as Marx has further shown, is a mutilation of man and an assassination of the peoples, for it excludes from work all that is specifically human, namely the planning of goals and of the potential means and methods of attaining them. Thus man is reduced to a human machine consisting of bones, muscles and nerves, while labour, the specifically human expression of man, is metamorphosed into an activity subordinated to an extraneous intelligence and subjectivity. It becomes a means, passively subservient to goals that are mysterious, unfamiliar and inimical. That is how Marx, in *Capital*, described the inversion of the relations between subject and object.

Work is thus no longer an inner need to create but a necessity for outward subsistence. It is no longer, as creation, the purpose of man's life but, as alienation, a means of 'earning one's living', while actual 'living' does not begin—or rather, seem to begin—until work is over, and then it begins outside work.[6]

As has been shown, the new scientific and technological revolution, by opening up the perspective of a 'negation of a negation'—by a new inversion, that is, of the relations between subject and object, between man and machine—confers on the subject, man, his primacy and mastery and, by proceeding beyond the antinomy between direction and execution, between mental work and physical work, invests him, in contrast to the nefarious dualisms of the past, with the integrity and plenitude that are his due.

## 2. *The Human Potential*

In order to face up to the unprecedented problems set by

6. When Marx spoke of 'abolishing' work it was in the sense of breaking with a system which reduces work to its animal form, depriving it wholly of its human character (notably the determination of its own aims) and making of it a 'natural necessity', extraneous to man (see *Contribution to the Critique of Political Economy*).

this mutation it will be necessary to eliminate a number of illusions and myths, beginning with those of spontaneity and automatism.

In the capitalist world, the myth that *the development of the productive forces would alone be enough* to solve the problems arising out of the new scientific and technological revolution without any radical change in productive or class relations—in other words, without the disappearance of capitalism and the principle by which it is sustained.

In socialist countries, the proposition which is the exact opposite of the above, to the effect that *a change in productive relations would alone be enough* to solve these problems once and for all and would automatically bring into being the new man, on the assumption that mere abolition of the fundamental contradictions of capitalism at the level of the economic substructure would suffice to eliminate the contradictions at superstructure level and to solve without friction the problems posed by qualitative changes in the development of the productive forces.

A. *In the capitalist world* the theorists of neo-capitalism, like those of reformism, are trying to assert that capitalism is on the way out because capitalists, the owners of the means of production, are gradually being replaced by technologists in leading positions in the economy and in politics. This is untrue, for the system as a whole is in no way governed by the laws of the technological rationale but rather by the laws of the capitalist rationale of which the goal is profit. Indeed more and more technologists are becoming aware of the contradictions here.

What a capitalist country produces is far from being determined by scientific or technological considerations (and still less by humanitarian ones); rather it is determined by the laws inherent in the market and in profits. The demands of the market are in turn governed by the demands of profit, for the public which constitutes the 'demand' is conditioned by advertising, while the system as a whole is governed by profit. The other sector of 'demand' is that of the State whose expenditure is determined by political options (military strike forces, war in Vietnam, etc.). The work of the technologists is organized in accordance with that extraneous goal and the rationale that goes with it.

In all capitalist countries major decisions are made by big business, the government, the army, or various pressure groups; the technologists merely carry out those decisions, though sometimes at a very high level.

A further illusion, complacently noised abroad by those anxious to preserve the capitalist system, is that, with the development of technology and productivity, capitalism is gradually becoming transformed into a classless society by the steady rise in the standard of living—a rise that is bringing about the gradual elimination of the working class as such.

But it is utterly false to maintain that there has been any real alteration in the unequal distribution of incomes. One has only to consider the United States, for example—the country, that is, where the new scientific and technological revolution is furthest advanced and where the income *per capita* is highest—to find the most glaring inequality. At the top, 20 per cent of the population share 46 per cent of the total income, while at the bottom, the least fortunate section, 20 per cent share only 4.6 per cent.

But this inequality in the field of income distribution and of consumption arises from, and indeed reflects, a fundamental disparity in the field of production where there is a radical distinction between those who own the means of production and profit by the surplus-value and those who have nothing to sell except their labour-power and who produce surplus-value for others. The latter category is excluded from all decision-making, being wholly 'alienated' from an extraneous, transcendent will which dictates its activity both in production and in consumption.

Thus neo-capitalism's sophistries about the alleged disappearance of class differences and diminishing class antagonisms are given the lie by historical experience: not only is there no numerical decline in the working class, and not only is the class struggle as real and meaningful as it has ever been, but the role of the working class (comprising non-manual and manual workers) is more essential than ever before. For it is the working class which, as the organizing and directing force of the movement, is capable of resolving the contradictions inherent in capitalism at the present stage of development of the scientific and technological revolution.

This becomes glaringly evident as soon as we cease to define the working class in the narrow sense, as comprising only *manual workers*. For this is a biased, unscientific definition such as Marx himself never had in mind.

B. *In socialist countries*, diametrically opposed illusions have held back and sometimes actually distorted the construction of socialism at home, while presenting to the outside world an image of socialism that amounts to a caricature.

The impoverishment and mutilation of the Marxist concept of historical materialism is at the root of this illusion which, by unduly stressing only one of the levels of the social structure, that of the productive relations or class relations, ultimately leads to the underestimation by those at the top of the importance of changes in the productive forces, and to a similar underestimation by those at the bottom of the possible repercussions of the superstructure upon the substructure.

This in turn has given rise to two major illusions. One is that, from the moment that the working class has seized power and has transformed the productive relations by suppressing private ownership of the means of production, eternal concord and harmony will reign between the productive forces and the productive relations, thus obviating significant contradictions and the need for perpetual re-adjustment. The second illusion is to believe that a change in the productive relations in itself constitutes socialism and that it will automatically lead to changes in the super-structure, namely to socialist democracy in the State, to a socialist ideology and to a new socialist man.

History has shown both these suppositions to be false.

From an economic viewpoint—and well beyond the time when [in the U.S.S.R.—Translator] extreme central-ization was demanded not only by initial technological and cultural backwardness but also by poverty, the capitalist blockade and the war—there continued to persist a bureau-cratic centralist system in which planning was carried out exclusively at the top, the units of the substructure (the enterprises) being no more than agents for the execution of directives from above. Now socialism, because its con-struction began fifty years ago, before the new scientific and technological revolution, has been stigmatized, as it were, by industrialization of the early type with its essen-tially quantitative models of growth and the 'mechanistic' organization of its administration. The cybernetic model of administration—the model, that is, which involves a feed-back of the substructure's reactions—is only gradually coming into its own. Suggestions or initiatives from below function only as a variable which is dependent on guide-lines laid down exclusively by those at the top.

Furthermore the enterprises were conceived as organisms whose essential relations were vertical (linked to the top, the planning centre), rather than horizontal (interaction with other enterprises).

In a structure of this kind, nothing is regulated by the market, that is to say by the real needs of the masses, since the central planning is based on criteria that are essen-tially political.

Nor, in such a structure, could there be any real partici-pation by the workers in decision-making and administration. It is true that the numerous meetings within the enterprises were, in the main, devoted to discussions about how to implement the plan, but only on the basis of the central directive which was not allowed to be called in question. Even suggestions as to detail did not go beyond the limits of the enterprise.

Such methods of administration have proved to be increasingly inefficient as the results of the scientific and technological revolution have made themselves felt. In a country such as Czechoslovakia, for instance, unhandicapped like other socialist countries by a heritage of underdevelopment and hence able to base her construction of socialism on the foundations of a highly developed economy, the first signs of deceleration and stagnation made their appearance in about 1961.

The search then began for a different model of administration which would render more flexible the economy's centralist bureaucratic system by giving greater autonomy to national enterprises and by reintroducing market relations between them.

But this first attempt to adapt to new conditions proved to be technocratic rather than democratic. Now, instead of dealing solely with the organizing statist centre, the enterprises began to establish 'external contacts' with the market but failed to set up 'internal contacts' with the workers.

Over and above this anti-bureaucratic reform it was therefore necessary to discover another model based on progressive participation by the workers in decision-making in accordance with the principles of self-management, a model whose economy would consist in organic units of production, these being not only autonomous but administered by bodies elected by the workers themselves. The units would be geared to the State plan by a series of relay centres both regional and national, the main preoccupation always being not so much to achieve a balance by way of inert counterweights as to ensure the lively interplay of initiatives from below and directives from above, thus bringing into being a form of true democratic centralism— a form in which democracy is not sacrificed to centralism, nor initiatives to the directives.

What we have described is in no way a concept inspired by anarchism or Proudhonian ideas of spontaneity. Every level would necessarily be controlled by the authority of a responsible administrator. But responsible to whom? Not, as under a capitalist régime, to the individual or collective owners of the means of production, but responsible on the one hand to the central authority (which, by definition, expresses the needs of society as a whole) and, on the other, to the workers' collective.

The fears expressed regarding this model of self-administration have not been substantiated either by the Czech experiment or by that of Yugoslavia, which started before the former and differs from it in many respects.

There are two main features which distinguish such a society as socialist:

1. The fact that work alone gives access to the appropriation of surplus-value and hence there is no possibility of exploiting labour;

2. The direct participation of every man, at economic level, in those decisions that concern his fate. As Lenin emphasized, socialism is not only a form of government that functions *for* the workers but one that functions *through* them.

### 3. *Scientific and Technological Mutation and Social Revolution*

There is an ideological obstacle which prevents both

capitalist and socialist systems from successfully coming to terms with the consequences of the mutation in a way that would enable them to ensure that social and political relations harmonized with the actual development of the productive forces. That obstacle consists in illusions concerning the spontaneity and the automatic nature of historical change.

We have indicated the opportunities opened up by the new scientific and technological revolution and have stressed how fatal is the illusory belief that this potential will automatically be realized. That illusion having been scotched, two problems remain:

As regards capitalist countries, how is revolution possible in a highly developed country?

As regards socialist countries, what socialist model will permit the realization of the fundamental goal of socialism in the new historical conditions created by the mutation?

To answer these two questions—the object of this book —we must recall the idea which is central to these reflections and which will serve as a guideline. For the first time in history the demands of economic and technological development and the demands of democracy and of human development are both proceeding in the same direction because economic and technological development increasingly postulates the full expansion of what is specifically human in man, his aptitude for creation.

At this stage of affairs an over-ambitious attempt to predict the future is all too liable to become a mere extrapolation of the past. We can be sure only of what is implicit in the development of the current mutation, and this provides us with the key to that 'possible' whose avenues it will be for our sons to explore—those sons who are already posing a problem to stagnant societies.

For thousands of years, right up till the present, each generation has been confronted by the general context of its life as by a 'datum' which hardly changed in the course of that generation's existence.

The young men and women who are now twenty years old are coeval with the new scientific and technological revolution. They are the contemporaries of a mutation which is transforming the general context of living to a greater extent than all the centuries of evolution that have preceded it. And so it will go on. Each generation will experience in the course of its lifetime a succession of upheavals bringing about radical changes in life and civilization generally. The young of 1969 are this mutation's 'primitives'. Who, then, can be surprised at their confusion and their revolt, and who will venture to blame them?

'Conflicts between the generations', which are now more violent than they have ever been before, are the inevitable result of the growing instability of the very foundations of our society.

In every society that has become embedded in the automatism of the past—even the recent past—in every society which attempts to refuse its youth the right to call in question its meaning, its validity and its goals, in every society that does not permit true participation by all its members in working out decisions which determine their fate, we find an explosion of delinquency, of lawlessness and destructiveness in young people who sense the absurdity of the system and of their own alienation.

Comparing proletarian with bourgeois revolutions, Karl Marx saw the former as having the capacity continually to transcend themselves:

'Proletarian revolutions . . .', he wrote, 'criticize themselves constantly, interrupt themselves continually in their own course, come back to the apparently accomplished in order to begin it afresh, deride with unmerciful thoroughness the inadequacies, weaknesses and paltrinesses of their first attempts . . . , recoil ever and anon from the indefinite prodigiousness of their own aims, until a situation has been created which makes all turning back impossible . . .'[7]

As historical experience has unfortunately shown, proletarian revolutions are not immune from bureaucratic sclerosis and self-satisfied dogmatism, nor yet from the perversions of Caesarism. But the new circumstances created by the present scientific and technological revolution provide for the noble and humane model of socialism conceived by Marx and Lenin conditions more favourable to its realization than at any time in the past. It is, however, a model that has yet to be realized.

The creation of a new cultural model will have to be an integral part of it. Where socialist countries are concerned, culture is faced by new problems. First of all, the problem of aims.

Today one of the outstanding characteristics of capitalism in the most economically and technologically developed societies, more especially in the United States, is that they are societies without goals.

Production for profit, as Marx has demonstrated, leads to production for production's sake, that is to say to anarchical production unrelated to the truly human needs of man, together with its hideous corollary—increasingly more in evidence as soon as the initial premises have been left behind—consumption for consumption's sake, the gregarious itch to acquire gadgets.

Socialism alone can offer an alternative, can create the human model of a technological civilization.

Not, like the Utopians, by arbitrarily assigning to society a goal that is extraneous to its history, but by actualizing its inherent potential.

'In the bourgeois economy of the corresponding era,'

7. Karl Marx, *The Eighteenth Brumaire of Louis Bonaparte*, in Marx and Engels, *Selected Works* (Lawrence & Wishart, London, 1968), p. 100.

Marx wrote, 'instead of the complete emancipation of human integrity we have its complete mutilation; this universal transformation into an object is total and, by a radical inversion, what is an end in itself is sacrificed to an ulterior goal . . .' Marx goes on to ask what will become of wealth when the form it has assumed under the bourgeois system has reached its limits. 'We shall see the complete domination by man over natural forces, both those outside himself and those within. We shall see the complete emancipation of his creative forces with, for its only postulate, the whole history of mankind whereby this totality of development becomes an end in itself.'[8]

Socialism is the first precondition for that inversion.

After an era in which all our needs and goals have been frustrated by poverty, the role of socialism, having freed man of the alienations inherent in all class systems, will be to satisfy the new needs created by the new scientific and technological revolution and first and foremost that major need which is emerging from it—the specifically human need to be a creator. In the lovely Utopia of his *News from Nowhere*, William Morris, Engels' friend, makes the man of the future say in effect: 'Now at last we are producing not for profit, but for the satisfaction of needs, for happiness, for life.'

This, then, is the new task of socialism. It must provide each and every man with the real opportunity to become a man, that is to say a creator, at every level of his social existence, whether economic, political or cultural.

This is as far as we can go in the definition of our needs, our prognostications being necessarily limited by the fact that we are beings enmeshed in the alienations of the past who cannot therefore know what will be the options, the criteria or the decisions of the men who will have left those alienations behind.

8. Karl Marx, *Contribution to the Critique of Political Economy*.

The problem here is to form generations of men who are adapted to the new modes of thought, of action and of feeling implicit in the present mutation, a mutation which involves the computerization of all aspects of life. How are we to shape men who will feel 'at home' in this new world of science and technology, men who will be able to master rather than be alienated by their own power?

The worst possible mistake would be to place man under the tutelage of the machine and to proclaim in advance 'the death of man' by throwing ourselves in the path of the juggernaut precisely at the moment when the cybernetic mutation makes possible an unprecedented expansion of human subjectivity.

Where exactitude is concerned, the superiority of the computer is overwhelming. The major problem now with regard to intellectual development is not one of attempting to emulate the computer but of controlling it, of devising problems for it and laying down its objectives. The principal virtue to be cultivated is not that of logic but of imagination—unless, of course, culture is to be reduced to a purely functional factor whereby the objectives are held to be already given and the computer is used to make the most of the means. The non-alienated use that man can make of that marvellous instrument of power, the computer, is to regard it as an intermediary, something that mediates between the vast mass of information and man's creative imagination. Unlike the nineteenth-century machine which reduced man to the function of a servant and a 'means', the twentieth-century machine can liberate him from all tasks except those of setting problems and choosing ends.

The new scientific and technological revolution demands in return the most radical revolution in human history. This is so, of course, primarily because the very objectives of culture have shifted. Henceforth—and this at the very heart of material production instead of at its periphery—the aptitude for synthesis, for intellectual growth and intellectual curiosity, once the prerogative of a humanist élite, will become available to an ever-growing number of people. The cultivation of the specifically human dimension of man becomes the first precondition for development.

Everything that art and religion had set apart from work or placed quite outside its scope thus becomes central to it, and not least the specifically human dimensions of subjectivity and of transcendence.

The mutation has, for example, compelled the most lucid among Christians and Marxists to conduct an exacting dialogue which has helped them, in the light of existing conditions, to rethink and lend depth to this specificity of man.

In the case of the Christians, though their religion had developed in them a concern for *subjectivity*, they had too often been led by a long tradition to reduce subjectivity to a mere inwardness so that their faith had inevitably become watered down into a purely personal form of piety. An exacting dialogue with Marxism has helped them restore to their faith its historical and social dimension, a dimension that is active and militant.

In the case of the Marxists who had, understandably enough, been led by the historical circumstances in which their doctrine evolved to lay the main emphasis on the objective momentum of historical reality and of the social struggle, subjectivity had too often been reduced to nothing more than an historical mirror-image of objective reality and of its movement. An exacting dialogue with Christianity has helped them to discover in Marxism—that of Marx and of Lenin—the vital role of the historical initiative of the masses, a role which owes its full efficacy to theoretical consciousness.

So far as *transcendence* was concerned, this was denied and, indeed, utterly repudiated by Marxists on account of the many irrational and thaumaturgic tendencies by which it has been bedevilled in the religious tradition. Yet the founders of Marxism had taught that truly human activity is other and more than the sum or resultant of the circumstances which produce it. A serious confrontation with the specifically Christian, biblical concept of man has enabled the Marxists to distinguish between the essential significance of transcendence and its alienated, obscurantist concepts. Thus they were able to delimit transcendence, not as an attribute of God, but as a specifically human dimension of man, as the emergence of what was new, and as the moment of the dialectical breakthrough.

In a significant reciprocal movement, Christians have been led to begin the disalienation of their faith, and to ask themselves whether religion is not in fact an alienation of faith. Increasingly they are coming to regard transcendence, not as a principle of order but as a principle of liberty, and to live their faith, not as resignation but as revolt, as a revolutionary rupture with things as they are.

This is only one example of the internal mutations demanded of doctrines and of men by the first scientific and technological mutation, a mutation which postulates pluralism as the principle of cross-fertilization.

In this way the whole problem of man and of his development is posed.

In a justifiable reaction against the formalism of the traditional 'humanities', which were in process of losing touch with life, there is now some reluctance shown towards any form of education based on the science of objective nature. From the great Cartesian rationalism to the petty rationalism of the positivists, the same downward course has led to the elimination of the subjectivity which is man's due, as though the subjective was merely a mirror-image or a record of an objective 'datum'.

Now it has never been more evident than it is today that we are, in fact, living in a world man has created, in a nature that has been entirely 'humanized', so that the first task confronting scientific humanism in our day is to help every man, during the long march of humanity, to recapture the moments of human creation which have gone to make that nature—in other words, to bring to life in each one of us in condensed form humanity's creative adventure in learning to know and transform the world.

Thus aesthetics, in the deepest sense of reflection on the creative act of man and on his condition, becomes, as the mentor of invention, an essential dynamic in man's development.

An aesthetic for modern times, that is to say an aesthetic of the great inversion, can no longer be based upon the Aristotelian principle of *mimesis*, the imitation of nature as it is. Rather, it must be what Brecht calls a 'non-Aristotelian aesthetic' based upon the 'distancing' and the inner creative participation of the reader, listener or spectator, who must pursue for himself the work's multiple suggestions, its problems and challenges if he is to work out various possibilities for the future. Such a form of art could be an education and preparation for the revolution that must take place.

For the problem is no longer, as it has been for thousands of years, to develop a certain kind of man adapted to the demands of a stable social order; rather, it is a matter of preparing man to develop himself and to continue throughout his life re-creating himself in a world that is changing incessantly and rapidly. It is a question, writes Radovan Richta, of 'turning the object of education into the *subject* of his own education'.[9]

This very suggestion implies a change in the *methods* as well as in the aims of education. If, increasingly, permanent education comes to take the place of school—hitherto responsible for transmitting a system of knowledge and

9. Radovan Richta, *Civilization at the Crossroads* (International Arts and Sciences Press, New York, 1969), p. 152.

for imparting the elements of an apprenticeship having, in principle, lifelong validity—if, furthermore, periodic refresher courses become more and more common, the existing principle of instruction would soon be reduced to absurdity by the rapid increase in the number of instructors.

For ultimately one half of the nation would be teaching the other half, while the need of the teachers themselves for refresher courses would heighten the paradox.

We should therefore envisage the use of mass media as auxiliaries in teaching and further we should envisage basic education as comprising, along with reading and arithmetic, the elements of cybernetics. In addition instruction should to a large extent be given by means of television and videotape, thus making available to millions of children, as well as to men and women of all ages, 'visual' lessons of the highest quality.

Only in this way can each and all be vested with the highest creations of science and technology, of life and the spirit, and be initiated into creation, created as creators.

Only in this way can each and all become familiarized with the problems involved in building the future; only in this way can they be kept informed, during the preparation of long-term projects, about questions, objectives, and potential options and variations of those options; only in this way can they actively participate in such preparation and feel themselves, as Jaurès once dreamed, effective collaborators in a universal civilization.

Such is the new man who must be taught how to be born:

a militant in the revolution against all forms of alienation,

a poet in creation as distinct from entropy.

## 2 The United States and the Consequences of the New Scientific and Technological Revolution

The new scientific and technological revolution cannot make a full impact without either a large concentration or a considerable accumulation of capital, and this for two reasons. In the first place because that revolution requires a close relationship between research and production; secondly because an undertaking cannot profitably be put on a computerized footing unless the combine concerned is of significant size.

In the capitalist world the United States provides the best subject for the study of the gradual transformations that are taking place in a market system based on profit, for nowhere else has there been such a profound mutation in the productive forces.

It would be fallacious to argue that, since only about one tenth of all production in the United States is automated, the country's economy and social system can continue indefinitely to be analysed in accordance with the categories of industrialization in the classic sense. Such mechanistic reasoning would be as absurd as for a doctor to declare: 'It is true that my patient's brain and heart are far from sound, but since those organs make up only about 10 per cent of his total weight I can virtually ignore them in my diagnosis and consider the remaining 90 per cent as being governed by the usual laws to which a normal organism is subject.'

This would be to ignore the fact that a socio-economic system, like a living being, is a structure all the elements of which are interdependent and that the consequences of the new scientific and technological revolution, in the particular case under consideration, extend well beyond the sector of computerized activities and automated factories already in use.

The entire socio-economic system is gradually undergoing a metamorphosis brought about by this massive invasion of production by science on the one hand, and by the mutation of the productive forces on the other, a mutation that bears no comparison with any that have taken place hitherto.

What, then, are the consequences for the United States of this new scientific and technological revolution which is giving rise to a 'post-industrial' society—a society, that is, in which the systematic organization of research and of scientific knowledge is tending to become the essential productive force?

The first and most decisive of those consequences in the United States is *a shift in the contradictions inherent in capitalism.* To keep on saying piously that 'the contradictions are intensifying' is meaningless without a rider to the effect that the contradictions in question are no longer those of the nineteenth century but those of the last part of the twentieth century. This does not of course mean, as we shall presently show, that the old contradictions have disappeared, but rather that they have been profoundly transformed by fresh contradictions.

What we have to consider, besides the new type of growth, are the transformation of the classes and of class relations, the new role played by the State and, finally, the ideologies that respond, not always very lucidly, to the problems posed by this insidious and abrupt metamorphosis as also to the painful inquiry concerning the final question, that of the aims of such a society.

What, then, is the basic phenomenon that will enable us to elucidate these multiple transformations?

The new scientific and technological revolution, *in that it demands long-term planning, necessitates an inversion of the relations between production and the market.*

John K. Galbraith, in his book on the American economic system, *The New Industrial State*, has stressed this essential phenomenon whose implications we must now investigate.

Where mammoth undertakings have been able to realize investments in order to computerize production, there is an increasing time-lag between production plans (prepared at research and development level), the commencement of production and the product's appearance on the market.

Since these new conditions make it ever more difficult to adapt production to the demands of the market, the latter must increasingly be adapted to the demands of production. There are two principal ways in which mammoth undertakings achieve that objective:

1. The conditioning of the consumer by various methods, of which advertising is but one;

2. The extension of outlets outside the market through the public sector's hypertrophy in respect of armaments and space research.

We shall be returning later on to the new forms of alienation which this inversion has engendered.

But we must start from the economic level if we are to discover the consequences of the new relations between production and needs. Under such a system, the choice of what is to be produced is determined less and less by the needs of the consumer and more and more by the demands for growth of those monopolies which control the market and condition the consumer.

Needless to say this new law which governs relations between production and the market merely expresses a tendency, as do nearly all economic, sociological and historical laws. It would be absurd to conclude from the preceding thesis that there is no longer any market in the

United States. Nevertheless it is true to say that the big monopolies, notably those in the advanced sectors of industry, are endeavouring with a considerable degree of success to become independent of the market. To such good purpose, indeed, that the development we are now witnessing—a development that is therefore the determining factor in analysis and forecasting—is the retreat of the market economy in the classic sense of the term, and the advance of those sectors in which the new laws are in evidence.

American capitalism in 1970 is not the same as the capitalism that Marx was able to analyse in England a century ago.

All the analyses in Marx's *Capital* were based on the theory of commodities, i.e. of production for the market, and from this derived his key concepts of value, of surplus-value, of crises arising out of the internal limitations of the capitalist market, and of the law of the relative and absolute impoverishment of the working class. His analysis remained valid, requiring no major modification until the early thirties of this century. Its last and most triumphant vindication was the great American and world crisis of 1929.

To maintain, as do dogmatic Marxists of today, that 'the contradictions are intensifying' without the qualification that many of those contradictions are new ones, or, conversely, to proclaim, as do anti-Marxists, that 'Marx's forecasts have proved false', is in both cases to place a scholastic and anti-historical interpretation on Marx's thought. Such an interpretation immobilizes that thought by encasing it in a system or catalogue of eternally and ubiquitously valid economic laws. But, as we have shown in the chapter on *Capital* in *Pour un modèle français du socialisme*, the essence of living Marxism, that of Marx and of Lenin, is the method that permits one, by analysing *present* contradictions, to foresee and realize the future possibilities.

In the present state of American economic development,

can it reasonably be supposed that socialism will prevail in the United States as a result of some apocalyptic situation in which the mass of the working class will be driven by misery to a rebellion similar to that of the 'Chicago commune' in Jack London's 1907 novel, *The Iron Heel*?

We have already shown,[1] in the course of discussions in France on the subject of the absolute impoverishment of the working class, that this impoverishment may be defined, not as a steady decline in purchasing power, but rather as the increasing alienation of the worker. This alienation is taking on new forms at the present stage of capitalist development.

The inversion of the relations between production and the market has resulted in the subjection of societies to the very apparatus which should enhance their power. When the needs of the individual are moulded, if not actually fabricated, by the producer organizations, and when the aims of the State are to a great extent determined by the internal demands of that apparatus (the 'military-industrial complex'), the new source of man's alienation and dehumanization becomes evident.

Man's labour and his historical goal in this way lose their specifically human quality, namely the consciousness of aims and also the choice of aims prior to the act of labour.

The question that is most tragically posed in such circumstances is the question of the aims of society.

Seen in this light, the objectives of the economic apparatus are objectives of growth and expansion. The growth, the efficiency of the apparatus, become ends in themselves. The only criterion of value is the criterion of performance. The only mode of thought is a functional mode of thought.

Hence there grows up a religion of means and a cult of growth. This trend in American life has been wittily sum-

1. Roger Garaudy, 'Fondements théoriques de la loi de paupérisation', *Cahiers du communisme*, January 1961.

med up by an economist as follows: Every citizen who presents himself at the heavenly gates will be consigned by St Peter to paradise, purgatory or hell in accordance with his answer to one single question: 'What have you done to augment the gross national product?'[2]

Though it has proved extremely efficient, this system has failed to resolve capitalism's initial contradiction, namely the polarization of wealth in only a few hands while large sectors continue in poverty. In the United States, of course, the proportion of the disinherited is smaller than in most other countries of the world, but it still remains a very significant proportion.

It is not true that capitalism, even at its most prosperous, has succeeded in overcoming that fundamental contradiction.

In 1900, 1/18 of American families owned 7/8 of the country's wealth.

In 1929, on the eve of the great crisis, out of 27,500,000 families, 6 million (more than 21 per cent) had an annual income of less than 1,000 dollars; 12 million (more than 42 per cent) had an annual income of less than 1,500 dollars; 20 million (more than 71 per cent) had an annual income of less than 2,000 dollars; at that time, and having regard to the cost of living in the United States, 2,000 dollars was considered to be the minimum required to maintain a decent standard of living.

The 36,000 wealthiest families had an income equal to that of the 12 million families each earning 1,500 dollars or less.

2. What is called 'gross national product' is the average value of services and goods produced during one hour of work, multiplied by the total number of hours worked in the country concerned. In the United States, for instance, an hour's work yields 5.20 dollars. 74 million people are employed in the civil sector, each averaging 2,000 working hours annually. This works out at some 150 thousand million working hours a year, resulting in a national product of 780,000 milliard dollars.

This is very far from being an 'economic democracy'.

In 1941, 14 per cent of families possessed less than 500 dollars.

To quote André Maurois:[3] 'Poverty, alas, had not been wiped out. The pyramid was not breaking down quickly.'

In 1961, 1/6 of the population was still impoverished; indeed, President Kennedy in his report on the State of the Union put the figure at 25 per cent.

In 1964 the economist, Leon Keyserling, wrote: 'I do not believe that the present system of distribution of the national income makes possible any substantial reduction in unemployment or any substantial decline in the number of the needy.'

In his book *The Other America*, which made a deep impression on President Kennedy, Michael Harrington points out that, in a country where private wealth and armaments take up 90 per cent of the national revenue there are 32 million poor out of a total of 200 million inhabitants.[4] He defines that poverty in its most dehumanizing form: the citizens of the other America are those whose plane of existence places them beneath any possibility of moral choice; so much are they submerged by their misery that the term 'freedom of choice' simply does not apply to them.

Since the country's social legislation affords least protection to those who need it most,[5] tens of millions of American citizens are deprived of social security and of a minimum living wage.

Some of the worst hit categories are the racial minorities (infantile mortality in New York is three times higher in Harlem than in white districts). The same thing applies to

3. André Maurois, *A History of the U.S.A.* (Weidenfeld and Nicolson, London, 1964), p. 261.
4. Michael Harrington, *The Other America* (Macmillan, New York, 1962), p. 180.
5. Ibid., p. 9.

unemployment and to slums—three million dwellings in the United States are shanties or hovels—most of them occupied by negroes. In times of prosperity unemployment has never fallen below 3 per cent, so that in favourable periods there will be something like 3 million unemployed.

The poor in the rural areas are even worse off. According to official statistics more than 50 per cent of low-income rural families suffer from deficiency diseases as a result of malnutrition.

The most tragic case is that of the aged. More than 50 per cent of those over sixty-five exist on an income of less than 1,000 dollars a year. There are 8 million aged agricultural workers who are not covered by any form of social security. In New York 300,000 poor are wholly dependent on public assistance. The existence of 32 million outcasts, both black and white, testifies to the distortions of an economy which allows a cancerous proliferation of false needs while failing to satisfy the most elementary human ones.

Yet the system has succeeded in integrating the vast majority of the working class and this has combined to further the objectives of growth.

On the evidence of American society alone it would be difficult to contest the theses of Herbert Marcuse on the integration of the working class. For that integration has been facilitated by the fact that American capitalism can, without detriment to its expansion, allow the majority of the country's working class to enjoy a very high standard of living thanks to the neo-colonial exploitation of Latin America and many other parts of the world.

Thus it would be false to speculate on a general impoverishment of the working class which would 'radicalize' it and drive it to take revolutionary action, such as might have been envisaged in the nineteenth century.

Though the possibility of further serious economic crises

can in no way be excluded, it would also be a mistake to believe that capitalism is necessarily proceeding towards the limitation of its own market, with dwindling domestic outlets as a result of the impoverishment of the working class. For in the first place that impoverishment is purely relative and in the second place—and this is the nub—new outlets can be created by means of public expenditure.

Since the thirties the regulation of global demands by State intervention, as advocated by Keynes, has become the rule. The increase in public expenditure has opened up a vast field to industry, notably through investment in arms manufacture and the exploitation of space.

In this way, as President Eisenhower himself pointed out, a conjunction has taken place between a huge military establishment and a vast armaments industry. Within that 'military-industrial complex' there is no perceptible demarcation line between the big private monopolies and the State. The objectives of the State are now identical with those of the 'complex', while the economic machine secretes the ideology of justification necessary to the subsistence and growth of the system.

Anti-communism, through fear and hatred of the Soviet Union, of China or of socialism generally, legitimates the most prodigious military investments. The arms race provides the big firms with ample justification for their imperatives of growth.

The banner of 'liberty' has covered, and continues to cover, many a turpitude: inside the United States, the McCarthyism of the fifties; outside it, from Latin America to Formosa and South Vietnam, support for the most corrupt dictatorships in order to keep open the market for capital exports.

Thus the State, in the hands of the monopolies, plays a crucial role. For it is the State which finances the scientific research that conditions growth; the State, too, is a customer. Sixty-five per cent of Boeing's business consists in military orders from the State, as does 81 per cent of Lockheed's and 100 per cent of Republic Aviation's.[6]

Thus, in the early days when victory seemed assured, the Vietnam war was welcomed with open arms by the big monopolies who saw in it an opportunity for profitable investment capable of sustaining the 'conjunction'. It was also welcomed by the military who believed it would furnish them with a training ground for soldiers who would grow adept in jungle warfare. The 'military-industrial complex' was living out its dream and there were not a few intellectuals ready to give theoretical support to the enterprise, thus endowing it with a 'spiritual aura'.[7]

The policies of the State are adapted to the requirements of the monopolies and its actions both at home and abroad are largely determined by what best serves their expansion.

To such an extent do the monopolies and the State share common objectives that not only do the big private undertakings influence the placing of orders by the State, determining even the nature of the equipment, but they are entrusted with contracts for what are virtually military missions, such as the installation of a base or the definition of a certain type of missile. This interaction, one might almost say osmosis, between industrial and State activities[8] is not

6. Michael D. Reagan, *Politics, Economics and the General Welfare* (Scott, Foresman, Chicago, 1965), p. 113.

7. After some years, as a result of popular resistance in Vietnam and the political and military setbacks suffered by America, this situation has been reversed; there is increasingly vociferous protest in the universities, the military have been forced on to the defensive on their own home ground, and industrialists have ceased to regard the Vietnam war as a highly profitable business: for the past three years, rumours of peace have invariably brought about a rise on Wall Street.

8. See H. L. Nieburg, *In the Name of Science* (Quadrangle Books, Chicago, 1966), which contains a wealth of documentation on this relationship between the American State and the monopolies.

only economic but political in character for, by maintaining lobbies and their own agents in the White House, in government departments, or in the Senate or Congressional committees, the heads of the monopolies can buy both legislators and laws—in so far, of course, as the big industrialists are not themselves in positions of power. A typical example was that of Eisenhower's Defense Secretary, Charles E. Wilson, president of General Motors in which he held shares to the tune of 2,500,000 dollars. Ingenuously he formulated the supreme law of American politics when, in reply to a question from the Senate committee asking how he could with impartiality handle contracts with his own firm, he made the historical remark: 'I thought what was good for the country was good for General Motors, and vice versa.'[9]

The formidable economic and technological machine functions for its own sake, its growth having become an end in itself. To this it subordinates the people, their State, their culture and their ideals.

What forces of renewal can there be in such a social system?

The conclusions of the best analysts of American society agree. Whether we take Ferdinand Lundberg's studies of the American plutocracy,[10] Douglas Cater's inquiry in his *Power in Washington*,[11] Arthur M. Schlesinger on *The Age of Roosevelt* (the first volume of which is entitled *The Crisis of the Old Order*,[12]) or the sociology of American power outlined by G. William Domhoff,[13] and different though these authors' points of view may be, a general law becomes apparent. For all these books show

9. Cit. André Maurois, *A History of the U.S.A.*, p. 289.

10. His latest book, *The Rich and the Super-rich* (Nelson, London, 1969).

11. Random House, New York, 1964.

12. The Riverside Press, Cambridge (Mass.), 1959.

13. G. William Domhoff, *Who Rules America?* (Prentice Hall, New Jersey, 1967).

that the levers of power—in the big monopolies, in the White House, in the Federal Government, in the House of Representatives and local assemblies alike, as also in the communications media, the army, the C.I.A., and the F.B.I—are all in the hands of an oligarchy that controls, orients, directs and implements the present American policy under the guise of two traditional 'parties' whose programmes are in the long run indistinguishable.

The only true opposition to the system, the socialist opposition, has always been powerless because it has been incapable of resolving the problems specific to the United States.

Its initial stage was one of millenary anticipation of a new world, without relation to the world in which everyday questions were waiting to be answered. It was a form of socialism that differed from pre-Marxist Utopias only in its positivist belief in the necessary advent of socialism. According to the first Socialist Party manifesto of 1904, their programme was not a theory of society that could be accepted or rejected, but rather a description of what, sooner or later, would inevitably occur. Capitalism, they declared, was already working its way towards its own destruction.

The leader of this messianic brand of socialism, Gene Debs, had turned dogmatism into a morality that repudiated all reform as futile, thus condemning his party to inaction.

The First World War, by transposing the doctrines of salvation and resurrection, destroyed these illusions.

The socialism of the thirties, that of Norman Thomas, was scarcely more realistic. While aspiring to create a Labour Party, Thomas had no intention of assuming any responsibility in a society which he rejected *en bloc*. When he refused to take up any position, even one of constructive criticism towards the New Deal policy with which Roosevelt was attempting to stem the crisis, he lost the support of the unions and the workers. With the Nazi aggression came further deterioration, for a number of socialists chose the very time when the future was at stake in the war to launch their 'third force' slogan. One schism followed another and the movement became fragmented into a hundred and one sects all still retaining one feature in common—an eschatological concept of socialism, a propaganda of final ends incapable of choosing the means available in the real world.

The American Communist Party, founded in the spirit of the Bolshevist Party, did not succeed in putting into practice the methods of Marx and Lenin in the conditions specific to the United States. It thus became—as, alas, did other Communist Parties—far more a propaganda organ for the October Revolution than an internal force for the regeneration of American society. It was isolated from a people whose intrinsic problems it found itself unable to tackle realistically, and its ups and downs followed the fluctuations in the political relations between the United States and the U.S.S.R. During the period of mounting fascist peril and the war against Hitler, the period, that is, between 1935 and 1945 known somewhat pompously as 'the Red Decade', the American Communist Party, though never a significant force in the country as a whole, did in fact succeed in exerting a not inconsiderable influence upon the unions affiliated to the C.I.O. and also upon the cultural world of the cinema and of liberal anti-fascist movements.

In 1943 the leader of the American Communist Party, Earl Browder, hoping to make use of this far-reaching trend (of which the American communists were a very real part) as a leaven for all the regenerative forces in the United States, endeavoured to effect a radical change in the Party's organizational principles. It is difficult to say now what might have been the prospects of such an initiative—an initiative that could have been decisive had it not rested upon theoretical bases, among them analyses of American society, that were too sketchy to ensure any real success.

Be that as it may, the change in the relations between the United States and the Soviet Union immediately following the war, not to mention Browder's full-dress excommunication by the communist orthodoxy, condemned the American Communist Party to play a distinctly minor role in the life of the nation. Not even the McCarthyite persecutions, so courageously borne by the militant communists and their leaders, could bestow enough prestige upon the Party for it to become the moving spirit in a movement of renewal.

The past few years have seen the emergence of numerous minor prophetic outcrops, Trotskyites, neo-radicals, Catholic Workers and the New Left—not to speak of the hippies who refuse to play any part, whether as workers or as consumers, in a world which they totally reject.

Before examining in detail the subjective reasons for the impotence of this socialism and its inability to obtain a hearing, we shall attempt to analyse the changes that have been brought about by the new scientific and technological revolution in the social classes and in class relations. Such an analysis might perhaps enable us to find the answers to two questions. Firstly, who can take effective initiatives such as would transform American society to the extent demanded by the mutation? Secondly, what specific form could those revolutionary initiatives assume in the United States?

Here we must take into consideration the fact that, with the great scientific and technological mutation, organized intelligence is gradually becoming the chief productive force; there has been a structural change in the manpower demanded by the economic system.

Galbraith has described this in striking terms: '. . . the manpower requirements of the industrial system are in the shape of a tall urn. It widens out below the top to reflect the need of the technostructure for administrative, coordinating and planning talent, for scientists and engineers, for sales executives, salesmen, those learned in the other arts of persuasion and for those who programme and command the computers. It widens further to reflect the need for white-collar talent. And it curves sharply in towards the base to reflect the more limited demand for those who are qualified only for muscular and repetitive tasks and who are readily replaced by machines.'[14]

The shape of Galbraith's urn represents a remarkable statistical situation: whereas between 1951 and 1964 the labour force in the United States increased by about 10 million workers, from 60.9 million to 70.6 million, it is significant that virtually all the newly created jobs were for white-collar workers. Between 1947 and 1965 the number of white-collar workers (specialists, cadres, office workers, salesmen, etc.) increased by 9.6 million. During the same period, however, the number of blue-collar workers (manual workers) fell by 4 million.

In 1965 the preponderance of white-collar over blue-collar workers amounted to nearly 8 million. This preponderance, which continues to grow, is the most striking feature of these statistics. In 1900 white-collar workers made up 17.6 per cent of the total manpower. In 1965 the figure had risen to 44.5 per cent.

At that time white-collar workers represented 44.5 per cent, blue-collar workers 36.7 per cent, service industry workers 12.9 per cent and agricultural workers 5.9 per cent.

The general trend shows a similar rate of growth among scientists and academics:

in 1900 there were 24,000 teachers and 238,000 students;
in 1920, 49,000 teachers;
in 1969, 480,000 teachers and 6,7000,000 students (within ten years the number of students has doubled: in 1959 there were 3,377,000).

14. John K. Galbraith, *The New Industrial State* (Hamish Hamilton, London, 1967), pp. 238-9.

One of the fundamental principles of Marxism is to regard as 'rising classes', as the destined leaders of the country, those social classes that are most closely linked with and develop alongside the *avant-garde* productive forces.

If, bearing these facts in mind, one again asks who can take effective initiatives such as would transform American society to the extent demanded by the mutation, it will be found possible to eliminate certain answers from the start. Unless we propose to persist in the illusion of a revolution carried through by minorities, we cannot count either upon the black movement (which represents 10 per cent of the nation) or upon the most deprived workers who represent an even smaller percentage.

The only force that could be a majority force in existing American social conditions is the working class in the broadest sense of the term, namely the class that is playing the decisive role in the present state of the productive forces and is jointly constituted by the white-collar workers and the blue-collar workers. This new 'historic bloc'[15] is the only factor capable of involving even wider social strata in a vast movement for the renewal of American society.

What is essential is to correlate the traditional labour movement with these technologists, cadres, non-manual and white-collar workers generally, only 12 per cent of whom at the time of writing are union members.

The traditional American trade union movement now finds itself in an impasse. Its character has long been ambiguous: on the one hand it has been an important economic force *inside the system* through constant intervention in the labour market to curb the greed of the employers, while on the other it has been a social force *outside the system* where it represented as best it could the opposition to the very principle of that system. The

15. See below, Ch. 5, p. 190 ff.

scientific and technological revolution, however, has affected the development of the American trade union movement in two different ways. Firstly, it has progressively atrophied the movement's social function. Because the great mutation has enabled the employer to increase his profits by a technologically induced rise in productivity rather than by direct over-exploitation it has been possible to rally the administrative organs of the trade unions and, in their wake, the main body of the working class, to the aims of growth and to the nefarious consequences these entail—the policies relating to armaments and war. This is why the mass of trade unions have supported the war policy in Vietnam. In those leading sectors that are rapidly expanding and already engaged in long-term programmes, an increase in wages is profitable from the employer's point of view if it ensures stability of manpower and continuity of production. Hence the board of General Motors anticipated the claims of the unions, proposing of its own accord a sliding wage scale based on productivity in exchange for a five-year contract guaranteeing a 'work truce'. (Giant monopolies derive an additional advantage from such an arrangement since it speeds up concentration by liquidating less powerful enterprises which, being unable to sustain the same rate of growth of productivity, collapse under the extra burden.)

The second effect the mutation has had upon the trade unions arises out of the first. Having been reduced to a purely economic role which they have in any case already played out by obtaining all there was to obtain through collective bargaining, their function inevitably becomes bureaucratized—the trade union becomes an organ of the system.

Thus integration and bureaucratization are two aspects of the present impasse. And this explains the recent attempts at creating a third trade union federation, as also the aggregative tendency that is becoming increasingly evident among white-collar workers, technologists and cadres.

Perhaps this is an indication of new orientations, but of one thing we may be sure, and that is that the conscious organization of the new 'historic bloc' cannot be effected simply on the basis of wage claims. That would only mean prolonging the process of integration and bureaucratization by which the labour movement has been led into its present impasse.

The clue to the matter probably lies in correlating *quantitative* claims (wage increases, shorter working hours, guaranteed national insurance scales, retirement age, etc.) with a new *qualitative* demand: that made by a working class which no longer accepts its exclusion from management or its passive integration into the system—a working class which refuses, in other words, to be denied its part in the decision-making upon which the future depends.

This could bring about its conjunction with the technologists and the cadres who are beginning to give forceful expression to that demand. It is a significant fact that in 1968, and for the very first time, the research workers at the Massachusetts Institute of Technology—where there is a greater concentration of 'grey matter' than anywhere else in the U.S.A.—went on strike for an unprecedented reason, namely to inquire into the purpose and meaning of the work they were required to do, into its military relevance and its social implications. The student movement—the movement, that is, of the future cadres—both in the United States and everywhere else in the world, is asking the same fundamental question, though the form in which the students ask it may sometimes be disorderly and anarchical.

Because America is, perhaps, more highly developed than any other country, that question could be the common denominator of the aspirations of the new 'historic bloc' that is now in process of formation. This seems all the more probable in that both the ruling class itself and the middle classes are losing confidence in their own values, as is evident from the turmoil in the universities attended by their sons.

If there is to be radical change in the United States, it will not be effected by the victory of one party or the other, but by a conjunction of those social forces whose common aspiration is to provide new aims for the system.

There can be no doubt that a primary role in that conjunction will be played by the engineers, the technologists, and the cadres, as also by a great many intellectuals, and this for objective reasons—namely, the new structure of the productive forces and the corresponding importance of organized intelligence. There is a danger here of technocratic perversion as the inevitable consequence of an irreversible development. However, as circumstances are now, there are only three possible solutions in respect of the control and direction of technologists and technocrats: either they can be tied to and dependent on a plutocracy and its profit motives, as today in the United States and other developed capitalist countries; or they can be tied to a planned economy in an omnipotent and ostensibly omniscient State, dependent upon it and upon the political options it selects without reference to the masses, as now in the Soviet Union and in those countries having régimes that are statist, centralized, authoritarian and bureaucratic; or, finally, they can be tied to and controlled by the body of the working class of which they would form an integral part while helping to shape and to clarify its options—a prospect opened up by the socialism of self-management in Yugoslavia. In that country, as we shall see, certain pitfalls are presented by under-development, but the experiment there may suggest democratic ways of effecting the transition to socialism in highly developed capitalist countries.

It may seem paradoxical to ask what form socialism

might take in the United States. Yet it is important to give some thought to this matter, not with the paternalistic intention of 'giving lessons in socialism' to the American people, but because here we have an extreme example of the problems arising out of the search for a specific way of effecting the transition to socialism in a capitalist country that is more highly developed than any other from the economic, scientific and technological point of view. Even if our conclusions are fragmentary and tentative, they could be highly instructive for us as Frenchmen and for our quest for a French model of socialism.

The first prerequisite for an effective revolutionary movement in the United States is that it should be autochthonous and should not seek to borrow models from other countries with a fundamentally different structure. In the second place, the opposition should not be purely ideological and negative; it should be critical but constructive and also pragmatic in the best sense of the term, in that it is based upon specific conditions, conditions which, being real and actual, can open up a concrete perspective.

The United States is at present experiencing the gravest political crisis since the War of Independence. The development and intensification of that crisis is taking place behind the cardboard scenery of presidential elections and mock battles between Republicans and Democrats. Millions of Americans—all that is best in the country—are asking themselves the ultimate question: What is the whole meaning of the system and the mode of living it implies? This great interpellation manifests itself in the turmoil at the universities with a student body of nearly seven million (not to mention the millions represented by these students' families)—manifests itself too at the very heart of the Establishment and also in the growing resistance of the working class to the trade unions' traditional forms of structure and administration. How is this 'Young America' to rally, how organize itself? How in so vast a country can these forces be coordinated and combined on a nationwide scale so that they can help to open up a new horizon?

The experience of nearly a century of ineffectual socialism demonstrates that it is not possible to attain this goal by means of imported models. The economic and social structure of the United States in the era of the great mutation in no way resembles that of the Russia of the October Revolution, still less that of the China of the Long March. It follows that so-called 'Marxist-Leninist' or 'Maoist' propaganda will achieve little more than the formation of splinter-groups. Marxism, we would again repeat, is above all a method of resolving present contradictions to produce a human potential. Leninism, Marxism's authentic successor, is the art of overcoming, in certain specific conditions, firstly national traditions, in order to specify the *forms* of the desired socialist model, and secondly the conjuncture, in order to decide upon that model's *methods*, its *type* being determined by the socioeconomic structure upon which the revolutionary action is exercised.[16]

Hence to be Marxist or Leninist is not to apply Marx's or Lenin's analyses to radically different circumstances in which they have ceased to be valid. Rather it is to make use of their method of research in order to define new historical initiatives.

In America's case there is an autochthonous revolutionary tradition. The emigrants who came to the country after 1607 were often rebels, belonging to what Dickens described as the second city. It is significant that the Declaration of Independence should include, among the natural rights, the right to revolt. The greatest of American democracy's Founding Fathers, Thomas Jefferson, considered that the Constitution ought to be rewritten every twenty

16. See Roger Garaudy, *Pour un modèle français du socialisme* (Gallimard, Paris, 1968), pp. 301-7.

years. He was the first theoretician of 'permanent revolution' in the democracy: 'God forbid,' he wrote, 'we should ever be 20 years without such a rebellion . . . What country ever before existed a century and a half without a rebellion? And what country can preserve its liberties if its rulers are not warned from time to time that this people preserve the spirit of resistance? Let them take arms. . . . What signify a few lives lost in a century or two? The tree of liberty must be refreshed from time to time with the blood of patriots and tyrants. It is its natural manure.'[17]

This could form the root of the revolutionary spirit in the America of our day—provided always that Jefferson and the Founding Fathers are considered in the same spirit in which we have treated Marx and Lenin. American society today bears little resemblance to that described by Tocqueville, and to invoke his *Democracy in America* now, in the latter part of the twentieth century, is to take refuge in an alibi and to camouflage reality with a myth. The democratic forms corresponding to an agrarian and largely egalitarian society are no longer anything more than a mirage and an alienation in this age of extreme and inexorable inequality, dominated as it is by industrial 'dinosaurs'.

How has this metamorphosis come about?

There is a fundamental phenomenon which has coloured the whole history of the United States and still haunts the very best of her sons with its nostalgia—the phenomenon of the 'frontier'.

To the European, a 'frontier' means rows of posts, barbed wire, customs, a rigid delimitation.

To an American, up till the end of the nineteenth century, the frontier meant, as Maurois puts it, 'a moving fringe between civilization and the waste land'. From 1815

17. Cit. Saul K. Padover, *Jefferson* (Jonathan Cape, London, 1942), pp. 155-6.

onwards many fled from a Europe of monarchical and feudal restorations and emigrated to America in pursuit of their dream of a world where each could develop according to his abilities and not according to the accident of his birth. Most found there what they sought—a terrain ideally adapted to equality of opportunity. The resulting nostalgia has given rise to a whole new imagery of freedom—a world where a man, gun in hand, can win his freedom by his own merits alone, where no doors are closed to him, where a free market is the principle upon which are founded all other human freedoms. Under the Homestead Act of 1862 every immigrant was entitled to 160 acres of land. A human tide swept across the country from the Atlantic to the Pacific and any man who was active and adventurous enough could hope to carve out his own empire. The frontier, that apparently limitless horizon, offered to every man, irrespective of his past or his social origins, the chance to escape from the servitude of the old civilizations and to advance as far as he wished into the wide open spaces. It is this form of equality for which every American feels nostalgia.

In 1890 the advancing tide reached the Pacific coast and the director of the Census proclaimed that there was no longer any frontier.

This, the end of the pioneers' opportunity, marked the great turning-point in American history. It was the beginning of a fatal reorientation, for to some it seemed that there was still a 'frontier' in the form of conquest and imperialism.

Within a few years, and under a variety of pretexts, the United States had annexed Hawaii, occupied Cuba, and had obtained from Spain the concession of Puerto Rico, Guam and the Philippines. There followed the deliberate partitioning of Latin America which became, *de facto* if not *de jure*, an American colony. The first stage was the despoliation of raw materials: Central and Equatorial

America came under the domination of United Fruit, Chile under that of the copper companies, while Venezuela fell to the petroleum industry. The second stage consisted in the export of capital which realized vast profits in the territories themselves by colonial over-exploitation of local manpower. At both stages American imperialism relied on local oligarchies and everywhere, from Nicaragua to the Argentine, imposed dictatorships of the most corrupt and servile kind. According to the level of development, the 'occupying power's' collaborators were the big landowners or the most weak-willed among the bourgeois traders and industrialists. In return for their collaboration the United States financed the upkeep of unwieldy military and police machines. 'Under a system of this kind', wrote the Archbishop of Olinda and Recife, Dom Helder Camara, 'the rich become richer and the poor even poorer . . .' The situation today is such that Sol Linowitz, one of President Johnson's closest collaborators and his representative with the Organization of American States, quoted almost word for word Che Guevara's thesis when he wrote that the United States would one day be confronted with a whole series of Vietnams south of the Rio Grande if they persisted in shutting their eyes to Latin American conditions.

Laws that are suitable for agrarian and egalitarian communities will not meet the needs of a society dominated by big monopolies. Yet there has been no adaptation to a world transformed by the progress made in technology. What reactions there have been were negative. The first anti-trust law was voted in 1890. This was the Sherman Anti-Trust Act which declared illegal all combinations affecting competition or commerce between the various states or with foreign nations. In 1914 President Wilson put through the Clayton Act which again prohibited agreements between monopolies for the purpose of fixing prices and limiting competition. From time to time these laws have been invoked and added to but they are 'toothless monsters' which have never seriously hampered the rise of the monopoly system and have become increasingly anachronistic through their concern to preserve the freedom of the market in a world of long-term programming, a world born of the new scientific and technological revolution. These laws are no longer applicable because it is Utopian to advocate a return to the market when the present state of technology demands ever larger undertakings. They are not enforced because they run counter to objective reality, to the monopolies whose power is constantly growing. If they were enforced the effect would be retrogressive, for it would limit the expansion of undertakings whose size is the necessary precondition for the development of research, science and technology.

What then can be the 'new frontier', the frontier of unknown opportunities and unrealized hopes which was the theme chosen by President Kennedy for his acceptance speech before the Democratic Convention? This 'new frontier'—a frontier that would create immense opportunities for the investment of capital—is first and foremost an internal one.

'Poverty', as Harrington has pointed out, 'is expensive to maintain'.[18] The colour problem cannot be solved by legislation. When the negroes are accorded civil rights this offers no solution either in the South, because of their economic dependence on their employers and masters, or in the North, because of their social position which forces most of them into working as unskilled labourers if it does not reduce them to unemployment. The only effective way to begin tackling these problems on an economic basis is, in the first place, to industrialize the South, not simply in order to provide employment but to institute class relations other than those of master and slave, this last a situation that persists in various guises wherever the system is

18. Michael Harrington, *The Other America*, p. 137.

that of an agrarian society. Here again the solutions in question are not imported ones but derive from national traditions. A striking example, for instance, is that of the Tennessee Valley Authority which gave new life to a whole disinherited region by the building of dams, the distribution of cheap electric power, the construction of fertilizer plants and the reclamation and irrigation of vast areas for agriculture and reafforestation. This improved the lot of three and a half million Americans, formerly condemned to retardation and poverty.

Another vast field open to productive investment is that of social amenities. We have not been alone in pointing out[19] the tremendous discrepancy in the United States between private wealth and public expenditure, a discrepancy that is typical of decadent régimes. During the period of decline of the Greek city state, and later of Roman civilization, the luxury of private houses contrasted strongly with the neglected condition of the temples. Present-day American society would seem to exhibit a similar phenomenon. Their schools, hospitals, stadiums, and cultural institutions (or rather the lack of them) are well below the level evinced by private wealth. The satisfaction of these social needs would both stimulate the whole of the economy and lend it a more human aspect. Here again there are precedents in the American economy, for capital has been mobilized for a common purpose before, although admittedly in time of war. In 1917 President Wilson told the nation that it was not an army that must be formed and trained for war, it was a nation—an impossible goal if all continued to pursue their own private ends. And so there was a period when two million tennis courts—the prerogative of the rich—were transformed into wartime kitchen gardens, when the roads at week-ends were empty of vehicles so that the fuel could be saved and

19. Roger Garaudy, *Pour un modèle français du socialisme*, p. 233.

sent to the Allied armies. Sixty-five million Americans paid out twenty-one milliard dollars for 'liberty bonds' which were launched under the auspices of leading film stars, actors and singers. In that same year, 1917, and despite the traditional horror felt by Americans for compulsory State control, the War Industries Board, presided over by a Wall Street banker, Bernard M. Baruch, allocated resources, determined priorities, controlled prices— in short, exercised what amounted to an economic dictatorship.

In time of peace far less rigorous measures would be needed to channel investment towards the satisfaction of social needs. And those needs, from the building of cultural institutions to the construction of motorways, would prove no less profitable than the construction of strategic roads in Vietnam or the subsidies paid to corrupt dictators in Formosa, Seoul, Saigon, or Nicaragua.

The brilliant success of the flight to the moon has shown what can be achieved, in contrast to traditional American individualism, by the rigorously centralized collective work of several branches of science and industry working as a human team; from this we see that nothing is impossible.

How, then, can there be any doubt about the possibility of solving the major problems—the problem of poverty, the colour problem, the problems of providing social amenities and of giving effective aid to the Third World, this last a point to which we shall return in our consideration of the impact of the new scientific and technological revolution on international relations?

Here we have three main sources of investment which could open up a new frontier for the 'Young America' in the sense of all that is best in its national traditions. It would result in a boom unprecedented in the American economy, an era of full employment and of one hundred per cent utilization of the country's industrial potential.

That speculation was not a new frontier was amply

demonstrated by the collapse of 1929, the 'black Thursday', 24 October 1929, which marked the beginning of the Wall Street crash.

Nor were imperialism and colonialism a new frontier, as is evident from the failure of the Pentagon and the C.I.A. in Vietnam.

The new frontier—and the proving of this is incumbent on an opposition that is not merely critical and negative but concrete and practical—will be discovered in the exploration of the three royal roads to investment and expansion; namely the liquidation of poverty and the colour problem in the United States by the industrialization of the South; the satisfaction of social needs by expenditure on social amenities; and finally economic and technological cooperation with the Third World and with the world as a whole, with no political strings attached and regardless of the régime in the country concerned.

No doubt it will be objected that the Federal Government would have to use strong measures if it was to bring about so drastic a reorientation in the national economy. This is, of course, true, but the endeavour, despite its herculean proportions, does not imply the state control and centralization so inimical to American tradition. Economic stimulation and pressure may well prove more effective than authoritarian regulations and directives.

Fiscal policy will one day have to play a decisive role by adopting measures so severe as to be actually fatal against non-productive enterprises. Advertising and public relations, for instance, should be taxed to the extent of having to redeploy and invest in other sectors. This would bring about a drastic transformation of the production-consumption pattern in the sphere of the creation of demand.

The most difficult but also the most urgent problem is undoubtedly that presented by the redeployment of the armaments industry. But without departing from the criteria of profitability it can be shown that with the capital invested in the manufacture of bombers destined to be shot down or grounded in Vietnam, the American aircraft industry could create commercial airline networks of unprecedented dimensions.

On the national plane it is even easier to establish that as a result of its war and armaments policy the United States government is utilizing but a fraction of its real potential where science and technology are concerned. The devotion of so large a proportion of the American potential to the armaments industry and of so much of the budget to the conduct of an inconclusive colonial war like that in Vietnam is as senseless a form of waste as was the slaughter of bulls in Rio de la Plata solely for their hides, the carcasses themselves being burnt.

This programme is feasible without undermining the principles and the fundamental laws of the régime. It would, on the contrary, make them fully effective by preserving, regenerating, and giving reality to those traditions that have contributed to the greatness of the United States. *This does not spell socialism but a purposeful capitalism.*

But it is perhaps the only way to bring about a profound regeneration and to open up the prospect of a creative future both for the United States and for the world: A path that leads beyond a society which no longer has any control over its own goals, beyond a people alienated from the imperatives of a growth that has become an end in itself; a path that leads towards a humanization of the system, so enabling all the vital forces of 'Young America' to join hands.

# 3 The Soviet Union: Birth of a Model of Socialism

To understand the reactions of the Soviet leaders when confronted by the new scientific and technological revolution and the mutation this postulated in the dynamics of the system, it is essential to recall the circumstances in which the Soviet model of socialism came into being.

Marx had revealed in *Capital* the general laws of the development of capitalism and the latter's inherent contradictions, his conclusions being drawn from an analysis of the capitalist system in England, a system then reaching its most evolved form.

There followed almost at once the first dogmatic interpretation of Marx's writings. This was the work of Kautsky who, in a spirit of positivist evolutionism, extrapolated the laws Marx had discovered and concluded that socialism could only emerge from a fully mature capitalist society which would automatically turn into its opposite. All the working class had to do was to prepare itself and wait.

Whereas Lenin resolutely led a workers' party along the road to revolution in a country still deeply imbued with feudalism and lagging a century behind England, France and even behind Germany, in the development of capitalism, Kautsky, who could not accept 'the minutest deviation from the German model,'[1] and remained tied to a 'servile imitation of the past', behaved towards the counter-revolution with the caution born of his dogmatic Marxism. Basing his argument on the postulate that a socialist revolution was only possible in the most advanced industrial coun-

1. Lenin, 'Our Revolution' (January 1923), *Works* (Lawrence & Wishart, London), Vol. 33, p. 476.

tries, he declared that in Russia 'the objective economic premises' for socialism did not exist, hence there should be no revolution.

Lenin answered in the name of a Marxism that was living and not dogmatic. Instead of keeping rigidly to the letter of Marx's teaching (as a catalogue of laws valid for the historical period in which they were discovered but extrapolated for all times and all places), the Marxism of Lenin held rather to the spirit of that teaching—the science and art, that is, of releasing revolutionary potential from the specific contradictions in a given country at a given time, and subsequently actualizing that potential.

As opposed to the irreversible mechanistic determinism of the 'orthodox' who clung to the classic example of the French Revolution—economic maturity followed by political revolution—Lenin demonstrated both in theory and in practice that this order could be reversed. He believed that the worst mistake revolutionaries could commit was to look back to the revolutions of the past, heedless of the fact that life is constantly introducing fresh elements.

In reply to Kautsky's objections he wrote: 'The development of the productive forces of Russia has not attained the level that makes socialism possible. All the heroes of the Second International beat the drums about this proposition. They keep harping on this incontrovertible proposition in a thousand different keys and think that it is the decisive criterion of our revolution. . .' To this he added: 'What if the complete hopelessness of the situation, by stimulating the efforts of the workers and peasants tenfold, offered us the opportunity to create the fundamental requisites of civilization in a different way from that of the West European countries? . . . If a definite level of culture is required for the building of socialism . . . why cannot we begin by first achieving the prerequisites for that definite level of culture in a revolutionary way, and *then*, with the aid of the workers' and peasants' government and the Soviet system, proceed to overtake the other nations?"[2]

The October Revolution gave a clear demonstration of that possibility. Thus the first breach was made in the capitalist system and the first concrete alternative to capitalism was created.

In directing and in leading that revolution to victory, Lenin never succumbed to Kautsky's error of dogmatism. He was always perfectly aware of the specifically Russian nature of the revolution as also of the features it derived from the conjuncture. In his writings he is always careful to distinguish between those things which, in the first socialist revolution, had universal validity and those that were determined by history or the preceding social structure.

In an earlier work,[3] as we followed Lenin's teaching step by step, we were able to show that, contrary to what had become dogma in the Communist Party over a period of twenty-five years, the principles of Marxism do not necessarily imply either that:

the existence of only one party is a necessary precondition for the construction of socialism; or that

the dictatorship of the proletariat must of necessity be exercised through the Communist Party; or, lastly, that

the socialist revolution necessarily postulates the limitation of the political rights of the bourgeoisie once the latter have lost their economic privileges.

If things took this course in the Soviet Union it was rather for historical reasons than on grounds of principle. To canonize these laws as necessary and universal is to substitute the thought of Stalin for that of Lenin.

2. Lenin, 'Our Revolution' (January 1923), *Works*, Vol. 33, pp. 478-9.

3. Roger Garaudy, *Pour un modèle français du socialisme*, pp. 118-24.

As regards the transition to multi-party socialism, Lenin was still able to write in October 1917: 'By seizing full power, the Soviets could still, today—and this is probably their last chance—ensure the peaceful development of the revolution, peaceful elections of deputies by the people, and a peaceful struggle of the parties inside the Soviets; they could test the programmes of the various parties in practice and power could pass peacefully from one party to another.'[4] It was for historical reasons alone, namely the successive adherence of all the other parties to the armed counter-revolution and their collaboration with the invaders from abroad, that the Bolshevist Party remained the only one capable of leading the socialist revolution to its victorious conclusion.

As regards the limitation of the political rights of the bourgeoisie, Lenin is equally explicit: '... the question of depriving the exploiters of the franchise is a purely Russian question ... One must approach the question of restricting the franchise by studying the *specific conditions* of the Russian revolution and the *specific path* of its development ... It would be a mistake, however, to guarantee in advance that the impending proletarian revolutions in Europe will all, or the majority of them, be necessarily accompanied by restriction of the franchise for the bourgeoisie.'[5]

Lenin in no way envisaged conferring upon the Communist Party the sole privilege of speaking in the name of the working class or of exercising a dictatorship on behalf of that class. Indeed, far from identifying the dictatorship of the proletariat with the dictatorship of the Party and claiming for that Party a monopoly in State power, he goes so far as to state that control by the masses *without a party* is indispensable if there are not to be bureaucratic

4. Lenin, 'The Tasks of the Revolution', *Works*, Vol. 26, pp. 67, 68.
5. Lenin, 'The Proletarian Revolution and the Renegade Kautsky', *Works*, Vol. 28, pp. 255, 256.

distortions: 'Our State', he writes in December 1920, 'is a workers' State with a bureaucratic twist to it . . . We now have a State under which it is the business of the massively organized proletariat to protect itself, while we, for our part, must use these workers' organizations to protect the workers from their State, and to get them to protect our State.'[6] One of the essential tasks confronting the trade unions—organizations which comprised, besides communists, large numbers of non-Party workers—should be, Lenin held, to combat 'bureaucratic distortions of the Soviet apparatus . . .'[7]

During the last years of his life, between 1921 and 1924, Lenin's chief preoccupation was to combat such bureaucratic distortions of the Soviet State, by which he meant the substitution of dictatorship by the Party apparatus for the dictatorship of the proletariat.

In February 1921, Lenin wrote to one of those in charge of State planning: 'The greatest danger is that the work of planning the State economy may be bureaucratized. This danger is a great one . . .'[8]

Again in March 1922 he wrote: 'Our worst internal enemy is the bureaucrat—the Communist who occupies a responsible (or not responsible) Soviet post and enjoys universal respect as a conscientious man.'[9]

Lenin realized very clearly that the chief obstacle to democracy and to the struggle against bureaucracy—which, in a bourgeois régime, is itself a product of the system— arose in the Russia of 1919 from the country's cultural and economic backwardness. It was necessary, he wrote, to combat bureaucracy to the very last until it was completely

6. Lenin, 'On the Trade Unions', *Works*, Vol. 32, pp. 24, 25.
7. Lenin, 'Once Again on the Trade Unions', *Works*, Vol. 32, p. 100.
8. Lenin, Letter to G. M. Krzhizhanovsky, *Works*, Vol. 35, p. 475.
9. Lenin, 'The International and Domestic Situation of the Soviet Republic', *Works*, Vol. 33, p. 225.

vanquished, but this would only be possible if the whole population took part in the country's administration. A little further on he points out that the low level of culture has led to a situation in which the Party apparatus has become the bureaucratized apparatus of State. It is here that he gives a prophetic definition of the Stalinism to come: 'The result of this low cultural level is that the Soviets, which by virtue of their programme are organs of government *by the working people*, are in fact organs of government *for the working people* by an advanced section of the proletariat, but not by the working people as a whole.'[10]

Lenin was fully aware of the objective causes of that distortion. In a reply to Bukharin in January 1921 he epitomized the drama of the Revolution when he described the working-class State achieved by that revolution as being distinguished by a population that was predominantly agricultural rather than industrial. The situation deteriorated still further after civil war and foreign intervention had virtually exterminated the best of the labour cadres all of which had been in the thick of the fray. This meant that the dictatorship of the proletariat had to be exercised with virtually no proletariat. It was an historical dilemma of tragic dimensions, for Russia must either emerge from retardation at whatever cost or resign herself to sinking back into it.

Lenin had both the genius and the courage to choose the first alternative, although all too aware of the risks this entailed. The gigantic task that confronted him was to achieve a primitive accumulation amounting sometimes to more than a third of the national revenue. Furthermore this feat, which no bourgeois régime had ever succeeded in accomplishing, had to be carried out in a country where industrial workers formed only a small proportion of a largely peasant population.

10. Lenin, 'Report on the Party Programme' (March 1919), *Works*, Vol. 29, p. 183.

The only instrument immediately available for the purpose was the minute Party apparatus, for if such sacrifices were to be imposed at the outset it was not possible to 'wait for consciousness'.

In addition to this fundamental difficulty deriving from the structure of Russian society in 1917, there were the tragedies arising from the events themselves—the disorganization of a war ending in defeat, the struggle against the White Armies and foreign intervention and, finally, famine.

To cope with this situation demanded military discipline and an extreme concentration of power. It was a matter of life and death, not only for the Revolution but for the country itself.

Paradoxical though it may seem this rigorous centralization in the assault period of the Revolution did not necessarily preclude democracy. By this we do not mean the democracy of privilege but that of the workers as a whole, for among those workers—even among the peasants, whom the Bolshevik government had freed from war and from their former servitude—revolutionary enthusiasm acted as a general corrective. The people lived, worked and fought in fundamental accord with their leaders. Lenin carefully nurtured this 'mass rising' of the new socialist democracy: 'The living, creative activity of the masses is the principal factor in the new public life . . . Socialism cannot come into being through orders given from above. It is foreign to official and bureaucratic automatism. Living, creative socialism is the work of the creative masses themselves.' Commenting on this circular issued by the Council of People's Commissars on 5 January 1918, Lenin told the third Pan-Russian Soviet Congress six days later: 'In introducing workers' control . . . we wanted to show that we recognise only one road—changes from below; we wanted the workers themselves, from below, to draw up the new, basic economic principles . . . We know perfectly well the difficulties that confront us in this work; but we assert that only those who set to work to carry out this task relying on the experience and the instinct of the working people are socialists in deed.'[11]

Lenin realized the need to offset the consequences of unavoidable centralization in the early stages by a sustained effort to stimulate and encourage the initiative of the masses. The maintenance of a happy balance between centralization from above and initiative and spontaneity from below was the first prerequisite for overcoming the difficulties of the first revolutionary assault and of self-defence against capitalist encirclement; for surmounting the obstacles presented by economic and cultural backwardness, by material poverty and, finally, by the lack of human cadres. It was the first prerequisite, too, for overcoming the difficulties arising from the fact that in the Russia of 1917 the revolutionary movement was confronted by a major stumbling-block, namely the mutually incompatible problems of the construction of socialism on the one hand and of the struggle against under-development on the other.

The fact that the first socialist revolution achieved success in an under-developed country has left its mark on the whole of subsequent history.

The absolute necessity to overcome under-development has led Lenin's successors to identify the objectives of socialism with the main objective of the initial phase of the struggle—accumulation.

If rapid industrialization was to be effected in the Russia of the twenties, a considerable measure of centralization was required. That centralization could only be rendered effective by political power. In the initial stages revolutionary enthusiasm provided the necessary political power

11. Lenin, 'Report on the Activities of the Council of People's Commissars', *Works*, Vol. 26, pp. 467-8.

which, ten years later, had turned into restraint and oppression.

The tragedy of Stalinism was to consist in a transfer or substitution of objectives; the ultimate goals of socialism were lost to view in the endeavour to realize its necessary preconditions.

The essence of socialism as conceived by Marx and Lenin was the liberation of labour-power. That is why Lenin was so apprehensive about the bureaucratization of the system and why he fought so untiringly for the deployment of the historical initiative of the masses.

The Stalinist perversion begins at the point where only one thing remains in view—the need to accelerate the development of the productive forces, with its inevitable corollary, the extension of the powers of the State, which thus becomes virtually an end in itself. It is here that the degenerative process begins, both for the Party and for the State, a process codified by Stalin in his book, *Concerning Questions of Leninism*.

As regards the Party, Stalin bases himself entirely on Kautsky's thesis, taken up by Lenin in 1902 in *What is to be done?*, the thesis that consciousness is brought 'from outside' to the working class. For Lenin this was only one of the components of his theory. After experiencing the 1905 revolution, he ceased to confine the revolutionary struggle's 'subjective momentum' to the Party alone, and by doing so enriched his thought. For him as for Marx there was another decisive component—the historical initiative of the masses.[12]

By discarding all moments of 'revolutionary subjectivity' except the Party which is alone seen as bringing revolutionary consciousness to the working class from outside', the first retrogressive step is taken: *the Party replaces the class in whose name it alone decides*. The Party in its

12. Cf. Roger Garaudy, *Lénine* (P.U.F., Paris, 1967).

turn becomes nothing more than its apparatus, the apparatus no more than its leaders. In an extreme case one man thinks and decides for all.

Here we have the very antithesis of Marx and Lenin. Instead of liberating ever greater social energies, the Party, followed by its apparatus and finally its leaders or leader, assumes the sole right of decision-making, settling all problems in the name of, but not in concert with, the working class and, in extreme cases, actually in opposition to it.

As a result of this shift in objectives, the Party and its apparatus put their main endeavour into the realization of the material preconditions of socialism through the administration of the economy. This was done on the basis of a narrowly centralized and authoritarian concept of the economy and the plan, a concept which, once again, is in direct opposition to Lenin's doctrine, propounded in April 1917, that the masses should be trained to take a general, direct and effective part in the administration of the State, for in this way alone could complete victory for the revolution be assured.

Thus the Party was transmogrified into an organ of the State and the decline of socialist democracy began. When State ownership becomes the only form of social ownership, when the economy as a whole is regarded by the leading administrative organs as a single gigantic trust in the hands of a constantly proliferating bureaucracy, when the programme is worked out solely from above, then decisions cease to be made at lower levels and the Soviets no longer exist as living bodies, both active and deliberative, created after the image of the Paris Commune. True, they still meet as a matter of routine but only to hear and approve reports and decisions made by higher authorities.

When the revolutionary ardour of the masses began to cool, the faults of the system were revealed. The governing apparatus of the Party and the State, growing steadily smaller and cut off both from the masses and from reality, became immured in subjectivism and bureaucratic voluntarism. As a method of governing society it was in direct conflict with the objective laws of development, while the actual theory of Marxism ceased to be the instrument for the revolutionary transformation of society, as in Marx and Lenin, and became nothing more than a means of retrospective justification for the rulers' actions, a mere apologia.

The system worked well enough during the early stages of construction, not only because, as we have already pointed out, the revolutionary ardour of the masses concealed and counterbalanced its faults but also because, in an under-developed economy ruined by war and intervention, needs were so great that the low quality of the goods did not inhibit their sale. Production, however vast and unbalanced, was necessarily absorbed.

But by the late twenties this kind of economic rationale already seemed inadequate. The peasants, far from showing any desire to be integrated into such a system of collectivization, took refuge in a farouche individualism.[13] The industrial workers, no longer called upon to participate actively in management, lost all interest in production and adopted the attitude of employees in an immense State machine or at best of resigned civil servants.

From then on the system, if it was to function at all, was obliged to exert an increasing degree of coercion. The end of 1929 and the early thirties marked a decisive turning-point when repressive measures were applied to peasants, workers and intellectuals alike.

In the history of the Soviet Union that turning-point of 1929 constitutes the same catastrophic alteration of course as did the turning-point of 1890 in the history of the United States. In 1929 the first stage of the construction of social-

13. Having for once in their lives enough to eat—under the Tsars wheat was exported even when the harvest was insufficient for the country's needs—they were consuming far more than in the past, to the detriment of urban supplies.

ism had been triumphantly passed. From the official *History of the U.S.S.R.* we learn that, as early as 1926 and in spite of the havoc wrought by war and foreign intervention, the economy of the country as a whole had reached the pre-war level. Russia's volume of industrial production rated fifth in the world and fourth in Europe. Within the framework of the electrification plan launched by Lenin ('Goelro') there were some striking successes: By the tenth anniversary of the October Revolution, in 1927, the output from the generating stations was two and a half times greater than the output before the Revolution. During the first five years of recovery labour productivity in industry trebled. When in 1926 and 1927 the Soviet government launched its first industrialization campaign the total growth of production in major industries rose by 18 per cent. No capitalist country had ever attained such a rate of growth. A new working class was in process of formation. In 1928 the number of workers and employees was close on 11 million.

The fight against illiteracy was vigorously conducted. Between the time when Lenin issued his decree concerning the elimination of adult illiteracy on 26 December 1919, and 1922, 5 million adults had learnt to read and write. The number of students had grown from 112,000 before the revolution to 162,000 in 1925.

By the tenth anniversary of the October Revolution the balance of successes testified to the superiority of the socialist system in overcoming under-development and in presenting man with opportunities such as he had never enjoyed before.

Only agriculture continued to lag far behind industry and the country's growing needs.

But the conditions had been created for another leap forward. In 1929 the Fifth Congress of Soviets of the U.S.S.R. ratified the first Five Year Plan, an exhilarating programme for the building of the economic foundations of the socialist society. The 'shock worker' movement, by setting an example of socialist emulation, perpetuated the 'great initiative' of 1919—that of the *subotniks*, who worked gratuitously on Saturdays in order to create the material bases of socialism. ' "Communist subotniks" are of such enormous historical significance,' wrote Lenin, 'because they demonstrate the conscious and voluntary initiative of the workers in developing the productivity of labour, in adopting a new labour discipline, in creating socialist conditions of economy and life.'[14]

If Lenin regarded this movement as having 'enormous historical significance', this was because it was the first prerequisite for socialism as well as a proof of the latter's superiority, for it permitted 'the creation of a new social bond, a new labour discipline, a new organisation of labour, which will combine the last word in science and capitalist technology with the mass association of class-conscious workers creating large-scale socialist industry.'[15]

And in 1917 Lenin had written: 'One of the most important tasks today, if not the most important, is to develop this independent initiative of the workers, and of all the working and exploited peoples generally, develop it as widely as possible in creative *organisational* work.'[16]

'Every attempt to establish stereotyped forms and to impose uniformity from above . . . must be combated.'[17] Emphasizing socialism's complete originality, he wrote: '. . . this greatest change in human history from working under compulsion to working for oneself . . .'[18] At the Third Congress of Soviets in January 1918, Lenin formulated the golden rule which defines the human greatness of socialism: 'The minds of tens of millions of those who

14. Lenin, 'A Great Beginning', *Works*, Vol. 29, p. 423.
15. Ibid.
16. Lenin, 'How to Organise Competition?', *Works*, Vol. 26, p. 409.
17. Ibid, p. 413.
18. Ibid., p. 407.

are doing things create something infinitely loftier than the greatest genius can foresee.'[19]

In this way, by invoking the 'subjective factor' of the revolutionary movement, he once again recalled that the free, creative historical initiative of the masses was inseparable from the conscious element, the theoretical moment whose expression is the Party's mission.

Lenin reasserted these principles at the height of the revolutionary assault period, a time which called imperatively for 'Jacobin' centralization.

Now the turning-point of 1929-30 marks the abandonment of precisely this Leninist dialectic, the abandonment of the complex unity between the historical initiative of the masses and the theory of which the Party is the bearer—the two poles, that is, of revolutionary subjectivity.

Economic development was well under way. Nevertheless under-development needed to be tackled more urgently than hitherto and the new tasks presented by industrialization, agrarian collectivization and the cultural revolution could only be carried out firstly by applying the specifically socialist stimulus of creative participation by the masses in construction, and secondly by creating the new preconditions essential to that participation.

Till now the centralization system had been necessary. Henceforward the 'Jacobin' centralism of the assault phase must be superseded by the initiative of the masses, an initiative given free rein by a democracy neither formal nor bourgeois but ensuring effective participation by the workers in the formulation and making of decisions, whether in the management of an enterprise or in State administration.

Yet now, turning his back on Leninism and its awareness of the need to adapt organizational forms to the cir-

19. Lenin, 'Concluding Speech on the Report of the Council of People's Commissars', *Works*, Vol. 26, p. 474.

cumstances and demands of any particular period, Stalin embarked on a series of measures which were to constitute the 'great charter of Stalinism'.

The initial problems to be solved were those of agricultural revival and agrarian collectivization[20] followed by the problem of industrialization.

Stalin elected to solve the first two by means of directives from above and of oppression.

In his speech before the Conference of Specialists on Agrarian Questions on 27 December 1929, he voiced an opinion on the subject of the collectivization of agriculture that was wholly opposed to the concept not only of Marx and Engels but also of Lenin. Stalin began by citing Engels' thesis from his pamphlet *The Peasant Question*: 'We are decidedly on the side of the small peasant; we shall do everything at all permissible to make his lot more bearable, to facilitate his transition to the co-operative should he decide to do so, and even to make it possible for him to remain on his little plot of land *for a protracted length of time* to think the matter over, should he still be unable to bring himself to this decision.' The quotation is immediately followed by Stalin's comment: 'You see with what circumspection Engels approaches the question . . .', since those he had in view were the 'peasantry in the West'. 'Can it be said,' he continues, 'that such a situation exists in our country, the U.S.S.R.? No . . . It is to be regretted that our agrarian theoreticians have not yet attempted to bring out with the proper clarity this difference between the situation of the peasantry in our country and in the West.'[21]

This passage by Stalin is of great historical significance

20. Agricultural production has been a recurrent problem ever since 1918. The N.E.P. had been one of the methods used in an attempt to solve it.

21. Stalin, 'Concerning Questions of Agrarian Policy in the U.S.S.R.', *Works* (Lawrence & Wishart, London), Vol. 12, p. 158.

for it is the first in which theory was openly called upon to justify previous decisions and also restrictive measures. It marks the beginning of the great inversion of Marxism which, from being a method of research into revolutionary action, became an instrument for retrospective apologetics.

It was a tragic situation. The kulaks (big farmers) obstructed the new policy by hoarding and concealing their grain and by organizing propaganda while leading the struggle against collectivization. In addition the rank and file militants, lacking political power, resorted to crude methods of collectivization such as their leaders had never really envisaged.

The old Bolsheviks were reluctant to apply to millions of smallholders repressive measures which might have been more legitimately used against a handful of exploiters. Hence Stalin proceeded to purge the Party so as to eliminate the opponents of those measures. Rykov, who had succeeded Lenin as head of government, was stripped of his powers. Tomsky was deprived of his leadership of the Communist International and the Politburo. Numerous leaders appointed by Lenin were eliminated and with them went thousands of old Bolsheviks.

After the purge, collectivization proceeded a great deal faster as a result of restrictive measures and constant pressure from above. In the course of three months, from July to September 1929, nearly one million peasant holdings were formed into *kolkhozy*—about the same number as had been collectivized during the twelve years since the October Revolution. During the second quarter of 1929 2,400,000 holdings were absorbed into *kolkhozy*.

Special repressive measures aimed at kulaks and saboteurs were now applied to 'middle' and even poorer peasants. 'In some areas the proportion of the "dekulakised" was as high as 15 per cent . . . violations of the Leninist principle of voluntary entry into collective farms were resented by the peasants, particularly the middle peasants.'[22]

In the belief that enforced collectivization would entail the loss of their horses and cattle, many peasants slaughtered their livestock, so threatening the whole operation with disaster. In 1929 there were 34 million horses in the Soviet Union; by 1933 only 16 million remained. More than half the horses had been slaughtered, as had 45 per cent of the cattle, a third of the pigs and more than 25 per cent of the sheep.[23]

The rage of the peasants reached such alarming proportions that urgent counter-measures had to be taken, but these resulted in wholesale departures from the *kolkhozy*. Because of the total absence of control by the masses the difficulties had to be met by means of directives from above, the methods employed being both authoritarian and bureaucratic. Progress was so slow that in 1953, when at last questions of decentralization and material incentives began to be posed, neither cereal production nor the quantity of livestock had regained the 1928 level.

In the field of industrialization the difficulties were of a different kind.

'When Peter the Great, having to deal with the more highly developed countries of the West, feverishly built mills and factories to supply the army . . .'[24] So runs the significant opening to Stalin's speech before the Central Committee on 19 November 1928. In that speech he discussed the problem of industrialization, emphasizing the favourable conditions afforded by the new structure of Russian society and the fact that only the proletariat, once

22. *History of the Communist Party of the Soviet Union* (Lawrence & Wishart, London, 1963), p. 443.
23. Ibid.
24. Stalin, 'Industrialisation of the Country and the Right Deviation in the C.P.S.U. (B)', *Works*, Vol. 11, p. 258.

its dictatorship had been established, could overcome that problem.

His evocation of Peter the Great was not fortuitous. It heralded an age in which nationalism would take pride of place, blurring, if not eclipsing, genuinely socialist motives. Indeed in the new, Stalinist concept of industrialization, autocratic voluntarism took the place of what Lenin regarded as a decisive factor—the awakening of the creative initiative of the masses.

Stalin decreed 'the end of spontaneity' where work was concerned and, while continuing to pay lip-service to Lenin's formulas on the role of initiative, enacted a series of restrictive measures which culminated in 'forced labour', euphemistically called 're-education'.

Proposed investment for the first year of the Five-Year Plan amounted to 3,400 million roubles which was five times more than the Commissariat of Finance had seen fit to agree. Having succeeded in imposing such material sacrifice on the country as a whole, Stalin believed that nothing was impossible and set his sights disproportionately high. In 1928 the Soviet Union had produced $3\frac{1}{2}$ million tons of pig iron. The Five-Year Plan provided for the production of 10 million tons in 1933. Stalin then began suggesting that the plan could be carried out in four years or perhaps even three, declaring that 'this level . . . of ten million tons of pig iron . . . is not sufficient . . . the output of pig iron must be brought up to 17,000,000 tons . . . in the last year of the five-year period.'[25] Militants and specialists, who held these targets to be unpracticable, on the grounds that they had been fixed without regard for effective potentials, were taxed with rightist opportunism and sabotage. In fact it was not until 1941 that the Soviet Union approached anything like the figure arbitrarily laid down by Stalin for 1932. In 1930 he demanded that pro-

25. Stalin, 'Political Report of the Central Committee to the Sixteenth Congress of the C.P.S.U. (B)', *Works*, Vol. 12, p. 355.

duction of coal and iron be increased by 50 per cent during the ensuing year. Yet when the time came he was forced to recognize that the real increase had been between 6 and 10 per cent.

It still remains true, however, that, unlike compulsory agrarian collectivization, enforced industrialization proved effective as regards production. Between 1929 and 1939 the output of electricity increased nearly sevenfold, that of coal and steel more than fourfold and of petroleum nearly threefold. In 1941 the total production of the Soviet engineering industry was fifty times greater than in 1913. In 1914 the schools were attended by 8 million children, by 12 million in 1928 and by more than 31 million in 1938. In 1913 there were 112,000 students at Russian universities; by 1939 they numbered 620,000.

But in human terms the method proved very costly. Certain features of this form of 'primitive accumulation' are all too reminiscent of the equally efficient 'primitive accumulation' practised in capitalist countries. This is described by Marx in *Capital*: 'These methods depend in part on brute force, e.g. the colonial system. But they all employ the power of the State, the concentrated and organised force of society, to hasten, hothouse fashion, the process of transformation of the feudal mode of production into the capitalist mode, and to shorten the transition. Force is the midwife of every old society pregnant with a new one. It is itself economic power.'[26] Marx goes on to discuss the frightening efficiency of this capitalist system based on violence and concludes his chapter on capitalist 'primitive accumulation' and its methods by commenting on the high cost of these victories, since capital 'comes into the world . . . dripping from head to foot, from every pore, with blood and dirt.'[27]

It is not merely out of sanctimony that we express the

26. Marx, *Capital*, Vol. II, Part VIII, Ch. 31.
27. Marx, Ibid.

wish that socialism might have achieved these ends by means other than those of Stalinism. The problem is one of efficiency. Hypocritical though it may be for the ideologists of capitalism, in view of the ever greater inhumanity of capitalist 'primitive accumulation', to deplore the initial cruelty that marked the construction of socialism, it is yet incumbent upon Marxists to ask themselves, not only whether the method used was the one that conformed best to their doctrine, but also whether it was the most efficient.

Now the absence of effective participation by the workers in the administration of the socialist economy is not only contrary to what Marx and Lenin held to be the essence of socialism but it also leads to shortcomings in the sphere of productivity and economic efficiency.[28] The imposition of labour discipline from above transformed the attitude of Soviet workers towards their work. Apart from the small minority of shock workers and in spite of the fact that the latter were held up as an example to be followed, the great majority felt themselves increasingly to be employees of a distant, faceless authority. To counter their indifference labour legislation was enacted which abounded in repressive and coercive measures.

During the early years of the thirties, industrial enterprises entered into contracts with the *kolkhozy* whereby the latter agreed to supply a given number of men and women for factory work. To comply with the agreement numbers of peasants were declared redundant in the *kolkhozy* and transferred to the factories.

Others who had resisted collectivization were sent to labour camps for the excavation of canals, the construction of railways and forestry work.

Finally the whole of the working class was subjected to coercion. 'Work books' were introduced by a decree of 20

28. This was not the only reason for low productivity. The great majority of the new workers were of rural origin and knew nothing whatever about industrial working conditions.

December 1938. Another decree made late arrival at the factory punishable by dismissal, and yet another, issued on 24 June 1940, not only declared absenteeism punishable by imprisonment but also prohibited any change of occupation.

The need for such measures is highly significant, having regard to the workers' attitude both towards the régime and towards their work.

The internal logic of that system, founded as it was on a view of an apparatus of Party and State that was omniscient and infallible, that spoke and acted in the name of the people although in fact imposing upon it directives from above, led inevitably to a radical inversion of the Leninist concept of the Party. In what was still called the dictatorship of the proletariat the Party supplanted the class, the apparatus the Party, and finally the leaders took the place of the apparatus.

In his *Foundations of Leninism* Stalin has canonized that conception of Party and State.

'The dictatorship of the proletariat consists of guiding directives of the Party plus the carrying out of these directives by the mass organisations of the proletariat, plus their fulfilment by the population.'[29] The mass organizations, of which the chief are the trade unions, are no more than 'transmission belts'[30] for directives from the superstructure to the substructure.

With regard to the State, Stalin put forward two theses that were in radical opposition to those of Marx and Lenin. The first was that the State may continue to exist even at the communist stage if capitalist encirclement still persists.[31]

This implies a concept of communism reduced to its

29. Stalin, 'Foundations of Leninism', *Works*, Vol. 8, pp. 41, 42.
30. Ibid., p. 34.
31. Stalin, 'Political Report of the Central Committee to the Eighteenth Congress of the C.P.S.U. (B)', 10 March 1939.

economic preconditions and heedless of its ultimate goal: the full flowering of all men and every man at a time when all restrictions and alienations imposed by the economy and the State have been overcome through communism.

His second and more deadly thesis, put forward at the plenary session of the Central Committee during February-March 1937, was 'that the class struggle would grow in intensity as the positions of socialism were strengthened and the Soviet State made further progress'.[32]

This thesis was a necessary corollary of the Stalinist concept of Party and State. For if the construction of socialism is directed by an infallible Party, every failure must be attributed to a conspiracy external to that Party, a conspiracy by the class enemy. This necessitates a reign of unadulterated terror.

And, indeed, a reign of terror was now unleashed, starting with a series of trials in which the 'evidence' was entirely fabricated. Thus the 'old guard' of Lenin's day was exterminated in the course of the years 1936 and 1937, at the very time when the 'Stalinist Constitution' was proclaiming principles in radical opposition to actual practice. At the very time, too, when Stalin, in the midst of a reckless waste of human riches, was making fulsome speeches about 'man, our most precious capital'[33] with ample quotations from Lenin on the subject of socialist democracy.

Ideology was increasingly coming to be identified with apologetics. It served to mask and justify repression in every field, in culture as in agriculture and industry.

The appearance of Stalin's *Dialectical and Historical Materialism* in 1938 provided dogmatism with its charter. Marxism, now in catechetic form, was here downgraded to

32. *History of the Communist Party of the Soviet Union*, p. 505.
33. Stalin, speech on the occasion of the passing out ceremony at the Red Army high school, Kremlin, 4 May 1935.

the level of eighteenth-century materialism, becoming a substitute for the old theologies and a Procrustean bed upon which science and creativity were mutilated.

In the sciences this dogmatic perversion of Marxism meant that the value of a theory was assessed, not in accordance with its ability to analyse experience and to suggest new hypotheses, but rather in accordance with its agreement or non-agreement with the catalogue of 'features' contained in the dialectic canonized by Stalin. The biological controversies, particularly on the subject of genetics immediately after the Second World War, threw a startling light on the damaging effect of these concepts which had wrought havoc in every branch of science, physics alone having escaped comparatively unscathed. For in spite of the pseudo-philosophical outcry against what was alleged to be the 'idealism' of the theory of relativity, of quantum physics and of cybernetics—this latter at first also termed a 'bourgeois science'—the exigencies and emergencies of the economy and of military defence meant that physicists were at least allowed to go on working, even if decried as idealists and positivists.

The consequences were serious in those sectors not immediately concerned with the requirements of practical life. Chemistry and biology in particular began to lag far behind. As for the humanities, they were even more ruthlessly stifled. An historian would be left to work in peace if he confined his studies, say, to the Khorasmic Empire or to Etruscan civilization, but should his interests happen to lie in a more contemporary field he would find his path strewn with obstacles, for since knowledge was entirely subordinated to apologetics even the destruction of sources was not eschewed. Psychoanalysis was held to be a 'bourgeois science'. The school of criticism and linguistics known as 'analytic', which some forty years ago began to elaborate the methods of structural analysis, was reduced to silence and many of its members were forced to emigrate, among them Roman Jakobson, Brik, Erik Eikhenbaum, Propp and Shklovsky. As regards political economy Stalin's word was law and commentary remained the only possibility open to scholars. From psychology to sociology, dogmatic exegesis spelt death to research and prevented the contributions and discoveries of non-Marxists from being integrated with Marxism.

The arts were an even worse case, not for lack of creative talent but because they were reduced to silence by a narrow-minded insistence on the utilitarian nature of art and by the mechanical application of dogmatic materialism to aesthetics. One of the chief sufferers was painting. In Lenin's day Kandinsky had been appointed vice-president of the Academy of Arts and the Vitebsk School of Art had been directed first by Chagall and later by Malevich, while Larionov and Goncharov were leading figures in the artistic *avant-garde*. Now all this talent was either forced into exile or reduced to ineffectuality.

During the twenties Meyerhold and Mayakovsky had opened up new perspectives for the creative theatre in Russia. But the Central Committee's decision of 23 April 1932 'on the reorganization of literary and artistic associations' put an end to 'the existence of groups centred upon these activities and opened the way for the consolidation in all fields of art of the creative method of socialist realism'.[34] It was a stranglehold that prevented any fresh attempt at innovation.

In the cinema, the heroic epoch of Eisenstein, Pudovkin and Vertov lasted a little longer, but even today creativity is still fettered by regulations. In the U.S.S.R. the censorship has banned the showing of Tarkovsky's tremendous film, *Rublev*.

Both in his novels and by his appeal to the Congress of

34. Tzapenko, *On the Realist Bases of Soviet Architecture*, Moscow, 1951.

Soviet Writers in 1967, Solzhenitsyn has disclosed the nature of this repression.

By comparing the facts in Khrushchev's secret report to the Twentieth Congress with those which were published soon after the denunciation of Stalinism and collected together by the physicist, Sakharov,[35] it can be seen that between 1936 and 1939 more than a million and a half Party members—about half the total number—had been imprisoned and that from 1936 onwards more than ten million Soviet citizens died in camps or prisons.

The year 1929 was crucial in respect of almost every aspect of the great retrogressive trend, both in cultural policy and in Soviet policy generally. Symptomatic was Lunacharski's dismissal from the Ministry of Culture to which he had been appointed by Lenin. Lunacharski's fine dream, 'the union of the artistic *avant-garde* with the political *avant-garde*', vanished into oblivion.

Such were the consequences, in every field, of 'Stalinism's Great Charter' of 1929 and the early years of the thirties. Later in that same decade they were to be punctuated by a series of bloody trials.

Those consequences were masked for a time by the tremendous patriotic movement unleashed by the Nazi attack on Soviet Russia. The national epic took over from the revolutionary epic and the great Russian people, at the cost of untold sacrifice, accomplished those exploits to which the world owes its freedom from fascist barbarism today.

But each time popular initiative subsided, the canker at the heart of the régime again became apparent.

Victory and the almost superhuman efforts of reconstruction[36] were followed by a wave of Stalinist terror not

35. Andrey D. Sakharov, *Intellectual Freedom in the U.S.S.R. and Peaceful Coexistence.*
36. As late as 1953-54 I was able to relive that 'revolution in

only within the Soviet Union itself but also in those countries which had just acceded to socialism. From 1947 onwards the Soviet Union itself experienced the elimination of hundreds of loyal Bolsheviks while, in the socialist camp generally, anything that was not a servile copy of the Soviet 'model' of the construction of socialism was regarded as 'objectively' revisionist and counter-revolutionary.

These crimes, perpetrated against socialism by the Stalinist apparatus, assumed three main forms:

The first was the export of the Stalinist political police who decimated the higher echelons in other countries as they had already done in the U.S.S.R. To this political insanity were due the trials of Kostov in Bulgaria, of Gomulka in Poland, of Rajk in Hungary, of Patrascanu in Romania and of Slansky in Czechoslovakia. *The Confession*, which is the testimony of one of the victims—Arthur London, veteran of the International Brigade in Spain and of the French Resistance, and a minister in Czechoslovakia—has laid bare the machinery of those trials. The accused, blackmailed by appeals to their 'Party spirit', were made to confess to faults they had never committed.

The second consequence of this bureaucratized centralism based upon a dogmatic insistence on the 'Soviet model' was the mechanical application of that 'model' to countries having a different structure, different potentials and a different past. This blind extrapolation led to some economic monstrosities. The system of compulsory industrialization, for instance, in countries where the objective preconditions did not yet exist, resulted in such voluntarist *'tours de force'* as the creation of Stalinvaroch in Hungary where a vast

---

the melting-pot' in the great Ural shipyards and also those at Khakovka and again, later still, at Bratsk, on the big Angara dams (cf. *Peut-on être communiste aujourd'hui?* (Grasset, Paris, 1967), pp. 36-40).

iron and steel complex was set up thousands of miles away from the sources of its raw materials, coal and iron ore. The Soviet 'political advisers' wrought as much havoc in the field of economics as they did in those of justice and of the police. Their centralist, authoritarian methods of planning, by exacting intolerable sacrifices from the people, led to the same result as had compulsory agrarian collectivization in the U.S.S.R.[37] twenty years earlier. They played into the hands of socialism's worst enemies by rallying the masses to the latter's cause. Thus by 1956 East Germany, Poland and Hungary had been pushed to the brink of counter-revolution. To prevent the restoration of fascism at the heart of Europe there was no solution —in view of the mistakes already committed—other than Soviet military intervention in Budapest.[38]

As has already been pointed out, the dogma of a unique model of socialism is wholly contrary to the teaching of Lenin who always drew an emphatic distinction between those elements in the October Revolution that had universal validity and those that were specifically Russian, between what derived from principles and what from history. Yet that same dogma was responsible for Stalin's excommunications and the consequent weakening and splitting of the communist movement. In 1948 Yugoslavia was the first socialist country to defy authoritarian dogmatism and to seek to build socialism in her own way; her leaders were denounced as counter-revolutionary agents, spies, assassins and fascists. Twenty years later the same thing happened again, in the name of the same postulates but in even more brutal fashion, for on 21 August 1968 Russian tanks crushed the attempt of the Czech communists to find a model of socialism that would be in accord with the de-

37. The only exception is Bulgaria where there really does exist a 'peasant party' which is an autonomous force outside the Communist Party; it has played a beneficial role.

38. See *Peut-on être communiste aujourd'hui?*, pp. 43-5.

mands of a highly developed society. Thus Brezhnev went one further than Stalin who at least never tried to invade Yugoslavia! He also went one further than Stalin in applying to a whole people and to its Party the methods that had been used during the trials in Moscow, in Prague and elsewhere. And today the Czech leaders have been forced by him into a bargain whereby they are allowed to hold their Party Congress only if they guarantee beforehand that that Congress will concede the necessity and the legitimacy of the Russian intervention. In order to obtain that result the composition of the future Congress has to be determined in advance by purging the Party's organism of all those elements which refuse to accept either the imposition or the importation of the foreign model.

It is significant that the occupying power and its collaborators should wish to extract self-criticism from the very men who, from January to August 1968 and under exceptionally difficult circumstances, sought to redeem the mistakes made under the Stalinist leadership of Novotny, the very men, in fact, whom they now also threaten with fresh trials. But Novotny himself is not asked to account for the gulf he created between the people and the Party apparatus.

Yet in 1956, after inflicting upon us, the old militants, the worst shock we had ever experienced, the Twentieth Congress of the Communist Party of the U.S.S.R. was able to raise the hope that such mistakes would not be made in future, that no more such crimes would be perpetrated.

By placing the mistakes and crimes of Stalin's period in their historical perspective, within the context, that is, of the painful but ultimately triumphant progress towards the construction of the material bases of socialism, the Twentieth Congress was able to open up prospects of a new future after setting an example of self-criticism such as no Party or State had ever provided before.

True, the manner of that self-criticism was strange, having been made *in camera* and on condition that fraternal Parties should not divulge its terms. Consequently our Parties were severely handicapped for, though we were in possession of a text of undoubted authenticity, we found ourselves compelled to refer to it as 'report attributed to Khrushchev'.

Yet the form it took was no mere historical chance. In a country where no political discussion other than on matters of official dogma had been possible for more than a quarter of a century, either in the Party or in the Soviets or anywhere else, any political change was bound to take the form of an explosion, as did Khrushchev's abrupt denunciation of Stalin at the Party Congress or, a few years later, his own disappearing act forced upon him without any prior consultation of the Supreme Soviet or the Party substructure, and wholly without explanation to the mass of Soviet citizens.[39]

Despite these limitations, the beneficial effects of that criticism were not long delayed. The agrarian problem, while still not solved, had at least been posed, and the frank admission that, at the time of Stalin's death in 1953, production was still slightly below the 1929 (and even the 1913) level, was the first prerequisite for recovery since it showed recognition of the earlier system's failure.

The dawn of liberalization within the régime promised greater freedom of opinion and criticism. This, together with official recognition of the necessity to admit material incentives and to effect economic reforms might, within a democratic context, have encouraged an increase in in-

39. It is significant that in Czechoslovakia where Stalinist methods were reintroduced after the Soviet invasion of August 1968, the Party's Central Committee (which had been considerably purged without reference either to the militants or the Party Congress) dismissed the President of the National Assembly in September 1969 and effected a complete ministerial reshuffle without ever consulting the elected Assemblies or the electorate.

dustrial productivity and have acted as a stimulus to creativity.[40] Russia's brilliant successes in the conquest of space and Gagarin's space flight which actually anticipated American attempts seemed to herald a third lease of life for the October Revolution and with it a decisive change adapted to the demands of the new scientific and technological revolution.

But the existing structures were so ponderous that they hampered and eventually paralysed the attempt to effect a regeneration.

Apart from anything else, criticism of the past was confined to Stalin's 'personality cult' so that its range was quite absurdly circumscribed. While it is, of course, true that Stalin's personality played some role, it should be seen as an effect rather than a cause. It was no more than the extreme expression of a centralized bureaucratic system.

Hence to make an issue of the 'personality cult' was to shirk the real problem and to create the dangerous illusion that a mere change of person would be enough to put everything back into order. The leader of the Italian Communist Party, Palmiro Togliatti, was then courageous enough to bring the true problem out into the open by showing that the perversion generally called 'Stalinist' was not due to its eponym's personality but was the inevitable consequence of the system. At the time he was publicly denounced by the Soviet Communist Party which declared that to question the system was to accuse socialism itself of being responsible for the 'cult'. What Togliatti was in fact indicting was not, of course, socialism but the authoritarian, centralized, bureaucratic model in the form in which it had been realized in the U.S.S.R.

The criticism begun at the Twentieth Congress was further circumscribed by the endeavour to preserve as much

40. In fact the annual figure was not higher than in previous years. See *Annuaire statistique de l'U.R.S.S. en 1962* (Moscow, 1963), p. 67.

as possible of the structures of the past. After Stalin's 'mistakes' had been denounced in terms that suggested that they were mere contingencies dependent upon his personal character, his chief theoretical work, *Foundations of Leninism*, was declared to be largely valid. This involved the retention of the Stalinist concept of Party and State, a concept wholly opposed to the Marxist-Leninist view and one which had been the theoretical basis of and justification for the entire Stalinist system.

The fundamental principle of this form of bureaucratic centralism consists in the dogma according to which the Communist Party and the State, as bearers of consciousness 'from the outside', must direct all forms of social activity, ranging from economic production to artistic and intellectual creation. Yet this was to ignore the other moment of revolutionary subjectivity, regarded by Marx and Lenin as dialectically indivisible from the first, namely, the initiative of the masses.

Such a monopoly in knowledge and decision-making may have been temporarily necessary at one stage or another of the revolution in a country that was backward, besieged, overburdened with material poverty and with a shortage of cadres. It can never be a lasting principle for the construction of socialism. Any system based on that principle will in the long run inevitably lead to bureaucratic, dogmatic and authoritarian distortion, to the degeneration of socialism.

The same thing applies to the Party. Where everything is decided 'at the top', by a ruling junta, the various Party organizations can play nothing but an executive role; at very best, they may comment on the central directives.

And indeed how could the 'substructure' validly discuss the course of events when it is deprived of all political information? To give only one recent example: On 21 August 1968 not one Soviet citizen (apart from the members of the Politburo and a few highly placed officials) knew of the Czechoslovak Party's answer to the accusations made by the members of the Warsaw Pact. With what can only be described as mistrust (not to say contempt) of the masses, the Russian Press, radio and television—and this, fifty years after the Revolution—disseminated only those ideas and facts that would serve to justify the Party line.

The same mistrust was extended to all the 'fraternal' Parties and their leaders. The opening words of the communication addressed on 21 August to the leaders of these Parties informing them of the intervention, contained the official lie: 'solicited by a majority in the Central Committee and its Praesidium . . .' Nor were the members of the Communist Party of the U.S.S.R. or the readers of *Pravda* better informed. They, too, were told the same official lie.

So nefarious, indeed, did this concept of the Party prove that here again Togliatti was led to draw from his previous criticism the further conclusion that 'a party of a new type' was needed. Hence he again adopted an expression of Lenin's, using it, in the spirit of Lenin, to mean the adaptation of organizational forms to the conditions of every country and every epoch. For nowadays a Communist Party, in an economically and technologically advanced country with bourgeois democratic traditions and in a time of peace and legality, cannot adopt the same organizational forms as those very justifiably worked out by Lenin for an illegal Party in an under-developed country emerging, with no period of transition, from a semi-feudal, autocratic régime.

The third fundamental limitation of the Twentieth Congress was Khrushchev's failure in his criticism to question —if he did not actually seek to perpetuate—the transposition of objectives whereby ends were confused with means, a transposition wholly characteristic of the Stalinist era. For the *means* that had been necessary in order to overcome under-development had gradually come to be identified with the *ends* of socialism. When, following Stalin's footsteps, Khrushchev gave the order, 'Catch up and surpass the United States!', it was an order that was deceptive in two ways. In the first place this goal was unattainable by the methods he advocated, more especially since the all-important 'cybernetic revolution' was hamstrung, and this largely for ideological reasons (at the time of writing the United States possesses over forty-two thousand computers compared with four thousand in the Soviet Union). To realize just how subjective and unrealistic such propositions were, we need only recall that, according to the plan put forward by Khrushchev in 1961 (and later abandoned), the U.S.S.R. was supposed to have surpassed the United States in the key sectors by 1970 and in all other sectors by 1980.

Secondly and above all, the goal of socialism cannot, even on the economic and technological plane, be that of capitalism with a simple quantitative difference. The achievements of socialism are not to be measured simply in terms of refrigerators and television sets. Its superiority, even in technological matters, must manifest itself in the satisfaction and creation of different needs that will permit the fullest development of man. *A new model of civilization must be created.*

Socialism cannot form a 'new man' without providing the conditions propitious to the birth of new *needs*. For, as Marx has shown in his critique of vulgar socialism, it does not consist merely in extending to the masses those forms of comfort, luxury or art once the sole prerogative of the privileged classes, but rather in creating new needs and new means of satisfying them, thus also creating unprecedented forms of happiness, of beauty and of life itself.

Thus the critique of Stalinism was intrinsically limited from the outset. Moreover the structures and the apparatus,

compounded by twenty-five years of bureaucratic socialism, were so heavy that they rapidly eroded all human
choice. The critique was never taken far enough to permit
a radical mutation and a new departure for socialism
which, once it had been placed on a sound technological,
military and economic footing, would have been in a position to reorganize its political and cultural superstructures
by raising them to a level commensurate both with the new
state of the productive forces in the U.S.S.R. and with
the demands of the new scientific and technological revolution. In the event, the present Russian leaders showed
themselves anxious to close the account and less than ten
years after the Twentieth Party Congress the critique of
Stalinism had been filed away and forgotten. These leaders, who constitute the essential armature of Party and
State, were themselves moulded by Stalinism and rose to
the top in Stalin's day in accordance with the standards of
the time: acceptance of the official dogma, the unquestioning execution at all levels of directives from above, and
the functioning of all institutions on centralized, bureaucratic and authoritarian lines. In 1966, at the very time
when the Communist Party of the U.S.S.R. was preparing
for its Twenty-third Congress, there seemed reason to fear
that the apparatus, already all too prone to neo-Stalinist
practices, was considering the possibility of Stalin's official
and ideological rehabilitation, for there had been numerous articles along these lines, some of them written by
high-ranking officers and public officials. It was then that
twenty-five leading artists and scientists addressed a letter
to Brezhnev, a letter which bore the signatures of some
of the most eminent Russian physicists, such as Tamm,
Kapitza, and Sakharov, and also those of the film director
Romm, of artistes like Plissetzkaya and, finally, the sig-
nature of a man who had played a role of prime importance
in Russian diplomacy—Maisky. The letter emphasized that
any return to Stalinism 'would be utterly disastrous', both

in the Soviet Union and abroad where, moreover, the attempt to restore such a régime would lead to a split between the Soviet Party and the Communist Parties in the capitalist countries.

There was, in fact, no official rehabilitation, but actions in the worst Stalinist tradition became increasingly frequent. A typical example was the decree of 1967, modifying Article 190 of the Penal Code of the Federated Soviet Republic of Russia which made the non-denunciation of a crime a punishable offence. After the trials of Siniavsky and Daniel, which were followed by that of Ginsburg, the Supreme Soviet of the R.S.F.S.R. extended these repressive measures 'by analogy' to include 'literary protest'. It followed that anyone having knowledge of such a protest was bound under law to denounce it, under pain of incurring penalties as rigorous as those attaching to the crime itself. From this we may gauge the extent to which neo-Stalinism has taken hold.[41]

It is hardly surprising that, in such conditions, adaptation to the new scientific and technological revolution failed to take place normally—in other words, in such a manner as to demonstrate socialism's inherent superiority. For by rights socialism should allow the productive forces deriving from that revolution to develop more rapidly than in any capitalist country and should, moreover, be capable of utilizing the revolution in the service of the full development of mankind generally.

The vicissitudes experienced by the Soviet economic reform are symptomatic of this state of affairs.

In view of the attitude adopted by the Twentieth Congress and of Khrushchev's denunciations at the Twenty-first Congress of the distortions and shortcomings of the

41. The restoration of Stalinism in Czechoslovakia a year after the invasion has similarly manifested itself in a ministerial circular that makes denunciation a national duty (Circular from the Czechoslovak Ministry of Education, 16.9.1968).

economic system, it would have been logical to expect a complete overhaul of the latter. There was, indeed, an announcement to this effect, beginning with public criticism of the inconsistencies and wastage resulting from bureaucracy and extensive centralization. The practical conclusion drawn from that criticism took the form of a move towards some degree of decentralization which, in principle, would permit decision-making to be entrusted increasingly to regional and individual initiatives (not, however, to the workers, but only to their leaders, selected 'from above'). Thus a new conception was emerging of the enterprise as a centre of accumulation, of forecasting and of management, enjoying much greater autonomy.

This presented, in all its aspects, the same problem as had been posed ten years earlier by the Yugoslav communists (who thereby incurred a full-dress excommunication); the problem, that is, of correlating the scientific requirements of planning with the autonomy of the enterprises and so giving the maximum scope to initiative.

At the same time, once initial poverty had been overcome, the immediate problem became that of the quality of the goods produced (in face of growing consumer demand), and also the problem of control by prices. The planning-market dialectic became a living dialectic which few of the leaders deigned to recognize. Yet a new socialist model of production might have emerged from this, marking a radical break with the capitalist model whose prime motive is the profit of the few rather than the needs of the many.

The decisions taken at the September 1965 session of the Central Committee of the Communist Party of the U.S.S.R. concerned two major objectives:

1. *To put new life into planning by giving greater autonomy to the enterprises*. This could have proved the means of putting new life into the role of the Party at the base:

the claim to bring everything to the working class 'from the outside' was beginning to recede. Questionnaires were distributed among the workers calling on them to make suggestions that might help to raise productivity technologically. Thus the basic organizations of the Party, too, instead of regarding themselves *a priori* as the infallible interpreters of the working class, might have been able to find their way back to the profound meaning of Marx's and Lenin's conception of the relations between Party and class by synthesizing the suggestions put forward from below, correlating them with the general demands of planning and supervising their application. This would have permitted progressive stimulation of the workers' initiatives, with increasing responsibility for those communists whose mission it is, on the one hand, to lend an attentive ear to the spontaneous suggestions of the masses and, on the other, thoroughly to assimilate new methods for the scientific management of enterprises.

And this more especially because the humanities, economic calculus and cybernetics have an important and growing role to play in the current economic reform.

2. *To make science play its part as a productive force.* Russian scientific policy is planned by a Committee for Science and Technology and by the Academy of Sciences of the U.S.S.R. That is to say that the scientists themselves are consulted about the organization of research. The first consequence of this is that basic research (which the capitalist countries have always tended to underestimate because it is not immediately profitable) is allotted a central role that combines happily with that of applied research.

Particular attention, for instance, has been paid to the development of the theory of elementary particles. Funds equal to the budget of a small state have been devoted to the construction at Serpukhov of a synchrotron of seventy thousand million electron volts and of an annular electronic accelerator generating six thousand million electron volts at Erevan in Armenia.

Space research with its study of the explosions of the galactic nuclei permits the observation of the processes by which energy is released, thus making possible an advance in the understanding of the structure of matter and also the discovery of new fundamental laws. In physics, a theory of solids is being evolved that will link their properties with their microstructure, while at the same time new and hitherto non-existent substances are in process of creation which, being harder than diamond as well as resistant to high temperatures, will be of considerable use to industry. Finally, the manufacture of the electronic computers so essential to the development of technology, the sciences and administration, has been considerably speeded up.

These combined efforts, stimulated by the current economic reform, have enabled the U.S.S.R. to attain a rate of economic growth of 8 per cent whereas American experts hold the view that the criterion of success for an industrialized country is a rate in excess of 4 per cent, an 8 per cent rate being achieved in capitalist countries (whose growth rate is necessarily uneven) only under exceptionally favourable circumstances.

This development of production is of vital human significance, for now we can see what has been called[42] a 'model of socialist consumption' beginning to emerge from the growth we have described.

Though the socialist way of life elicited new needs and a demand for consumer goods of a different kind from those produced in capitalist countries, the production of such goods was long hampered by poverty and the tremendous effort required to combat under-development. Only quite

42. See the article by J. Dessau, 'Vers la maîtrise de l'économie socialiste' in *Economie et politique*, Vol. 160, November 1967.

recently, as Jan Dessau has pointed out, has a consumer model as such begun to emerge.

There is no sign here of the unhealthy and anarchical hypertrophy of consumer demand such as is engendered in Western countries by advertising and by a style of life calculated to promote the flow of those goods most profitable to capitalist producers. Rather we see the beginnings of a tendency to stimulate consumption that is based upon quite different criteria—criteria that are either determined by scientific factors, for instance nutrition and health, or else inspired by a truly socialist concept of the world and of man in such fields as education, culture and sport.

Again, in contrast to the consumer model in the United States—where, as in other capitalist countries, there is a deliberate brake on 'social consumption' (e.g. parks, cultural institutions, community centres and crèches)—the Soviet model rates this aspect of consumption very high.

Finally, the price of individual cultural products such as books, records, musical instruments and sports equipment is kept very low so that they may be accessible to all.

The dominant feature of this future consumer model is thus primarily the stimulation and satisfaction of cultural and social needs, so creating the preconditions for the specifically human development of man.

Here we have the premises for the birth of the 'new man' whose needs would be created, not to accord with the demands of the law that governs the personal profit of those who produce the goods, but to accord rather with the needs historically defined by the possibilities inherent in the development of the productive forces, by the creation of productive and, more generally, of social relations that are no longer based on the individualism of competition and its jungle warfare, but on the new ethics of a society tending towards the conscious mastery of its fate.

It is, in itself, an irreversible trend, if only by reason of the pressure exerted by the new scientific revolution, but in the U.S.S.R. it is being continuously hampered and held back by the actions of the Soviet leaders now in power.

The inner logic of the economic reform, postulating as it does greater autonomy for the enterprises and for local and regional bodies and also an ever wider scope for individual initiative, has as its precondition and consequence, increasing democratization on every plane of social activity, more especially at the political and cultural levels.

But there still remains a very considerable gap between the requirements of economic reform on the one hand and political structures on the other. Marx, in analysing the 'bureaucratism' secreted by the capitalist system has shown that the principle in accordance with which 'the masters know best' and 'only the ruling circles, well versed in administering things, can pass judgement', is an ideology that derived from officials whose position inclined them to confuse the common interests of society with the power of the State they represented.

The socialist model which renders 'collective ownership' of the means of production as 'State ownership'—'State' meaning here a centralized State which disposes of the surplus-value and of all social work—has led to the fundamental distortion once so lucidly described by Lenin (see above, p. 82): socialism that is constructed *for* the people and not *by* the people.

Now while it is conceivable that these methods could be used to construct the material bases of socialism at an early stage in a revolution whose success depended on the swift elimination of certain backward conditions, it is quite inconceivable that socialism itself should be thus constructed, for its essence is the liberation of the worker, not only from the exploitation of the ruling classes, but from all forms of economic, political and spiritual alienation.

And that demands the creative participation of everyone at all levels of social activity.

If such a reform, with all its political implications, is to be fully and effectively implemented, this postulates complete intellectual freedom comprising three essential options: freedom to collect and transmit information; the right of free discussion, without fear of any sanction other than criticism of the opinions put forward; the end of restrictions imposed either by the power of the State or by myths instilled by one-sided propaganda and mass 'conditioning'.

Unless this stipulation is fulfilled there can be neither a democratic nor a scientific method.

In this respect the behaviour of the present leaders of the Soviet Union is significant. For now that, after fifty years of socialism, new generations of non-manual workers have arisen, recruited from the working class and conscious of their deep solidarity with that class with which they are, for the most part, integrally united, it is paradoxical to be told over and over again that non-manual workers must subordinate themselves to a working class of which, in the U.S.S.R., they have already long been members. What these declarations in fact demand is the subordination of non-manual workers (as, indeed, of the working class) to the central Party apparatus and to its officials who regard themselves as the infallible interpreters of the consciousness of a working class which is theoretically in power but which, since, 'harmony is pre-established', is never consulted.

This bureaucratic, centralized and authoritarian conception was and is the main obstacle to the realization of the economic reform, to political democratization and to the liberation of culture.

The substitution of economic methods of management for administrative ones was, in itself, a definite sign of progress. It implied a change of method both in production planning and in workers' incentive schemes. Regulations imposed from above were to be reduced, while trading between enterprises within the framework of the market was to be allowed largely, if not entirely, to take the place of centralized State control. In fact, where the means of production are concerned, the process of substituting normal wholesale trading for the centralized distribution of supplies is proving far too slow and the system of incentives, because of its extreme complexity, has been only moderately successful.

The fundamental problem here is the discrepancy between the proposed reform of the enterprises and the methods of the principal State agencies which continue to work along the old lines.

So much have things been held back during the past few years that stockbreeding and agricultural production in general have shown a fall-off as compared with the earlier period, while the rate of industrial growth is declining, especially in key sectors such as cement and iron and steel. Moreover, the United States has won the race to the moon whereas only ten years earlier the U.S.S.R. had been well in the lead with Gagarin's first space flight.

It is becoming increasingly evident that the centralized and authoritarian system, although efficacious enough in the early stages of socialist construction, has grown outdated and irrational in the present state of development of the productive forces.

One of the major manifestations of the new scientific and technological revolution as opposed to the 'industrial period' is that it demands an increasing number of centres of decision as also widespread development of the workers' creative initiative—in other words an explosion of subjectivity.

Only socialism would be able to fulfil these conditions, but if it is to do so it will have to be careful constantly to readjust social relations as a whole to the demands of the great scientific and technological mutations.

The present Soviet leaders, however, are an obstacle not only to those changes that are essential in the Soviet Union, but also to every attempt on the part of Communist Parties elsewhere—more especially in socialist countries—to seek models of socialism adapted to their own social structure and national history.

As in Stalin's day, published texts are the converse of the policy actually pursued. Over and over again we are told that there is no leading Party and that each Party can make autonomous decisions, freely choosing its way to socialism, etc. But what do we see in practice?—The boycott and excommunication of Yugoslavia in 1948, the broken agreement with China and the cessation of aid to her in 1960, and in 1968 the invasion of Czechoslovakia.

The true reasons for the invasion were stated quite explicitly in the Russian Press. Unable to discover any shadow of evidence of 'counter-revolutionary activity' likely to endanger socialism in Czechoslovakia, *Pravda* soon revealed that *Soviet tanks had not gone to Prague to fight counter-revolutionaries. They had gone there to bring the Czech communists into line.* What was significant, moreover, was the arrest of the Party leaders as soon as the troops entered Prague. *Pravda* of 24 August 1968 revealed the crux of the matter:

'The fundamental Leninist principle of the Party, the principle, that is, of democratic centralism, had virtually been denied.' In Brezhnev's view, this was to undermine 'the Party's leading role'.

Now the 'practical' measures in fact taken by the Czechoslovak Communist Party between January and August 1968 can be summed up under three headings:

1. The suppression of censorship so as to establish freedom of opinion.

2. The creation of 'workers' councils' in the enterprises so that at the economic level every man should then be able to participate at his place of work in the decision-making upon which his future depends and thus become, in accordance with Marx's fundamental precept, the subject rather than the object of history.

3. The modification of the Party statutes so as to eliminate the structures and practices inherited from Stalin and Novotny. In essence the new statutes aimed at giving every militant the chance to take part in working out the Party line. While condemning the formation of 'factions' as detrimental to the unity and hence the efficacity of a Communist Party, the statutes envisaged a number of measures intended to prevent a return to Stalinist theory and practice. These were:

*a*) To put an end to the identification of Party and State by prohibiting the tenure of more than one leading post in either Party or State;

*b*) The recognition of the rights of the minority which must not be silenced but allowed to voice its opinions in the Party Press, thus making possible free emulation in political and theoretical initiatives and consequently the Party's evolution by means other than explosions or 'palace revolutions' (such as, for instance, the eviction of Khrushchev);

*c*) To institute a secret ballot at all levels for the election of Party leaders;

*d*) To guarantee control of the activities both of the Party and of its leading agencies by publishing the Central Committee's reports and by suppressing any form of censorship, whether direct or indirect, by the apparatus actually in power.

It was this return to Lenin's principle of a centralized democracy in which democracy is not eliminated by centralism—a principle that had been systematically violated by Stalin and his successors—that was designated by Brezhnev and *Pravda* as the negation of centralized democracy and the abdication of the Party's leading role. Soviet tanks entered Prague to prevent any further indictment of the Stalinist interpretation and the risk of contagion in other socialist countries that this would involve, and also to obviate the threat it would constitute to those countries' bureaucratic machinery. And for the same reason Soviet pressure, varying in method according to circumstances, is now being applied to all Communist Parties.

That is why it is not enough to reprobate the military character of the intervention; we must also be clearly aware of the underlying theoretical and political principles which we must not hesitate to unmask and combat. The struggle is one of principle, for any return to the methods prevailing before the Twentieth Congress of the Communist Party of the U.S.S.R. or any concession, however slight, to a policy of restalinization would mean bankruptcy for the Communist Parties. Today the choice is a clear one: either a broad mass policy which alone would be able to rally all the pro-socialist forces so as to establish socialism in our country, or else alignment with the present Soviet leaders and their ideas, ideas which are incompatible with the fundamental democratic prerequisites for the victory and construction of socialism in highly developed countries. Communist Parties who choose the latter course are almost certainly doomed to become minor sects devoting themselves to the propagation of a model of socialism put forward as the only possible one, though in fact it bears no relation whatever to the needs and aspirations of the different peoples.

It is this crucial choice which constitutes the great turning-point of socialism today. The future of the Communist Parties depends on their ability to form a concept of democratic centralism, as also of the leading role of the Party, that is in keeping with the spirit of Marx and Lenin rather than with that of Stalin and Brezhnev.

The ultimate effect of the intervention in Czechoslovakia and of the pressure put on the fraternal Parties has been a very considerable debilitation of the socialist camp and it is hard to understand how self-adulatory texts can be published denying this debilitation and proclaiming that the Moscow Conference of June 1969 'constitutes an important stage on the road to the reinforcement of the unity of the Communist Parties'.

It needs little perspicacity to realize that such optimism is totally unjustified. What the Conference in fact reveals is the full measure of the crisis in which the international communist movement finds itself involved.

In November 1960 the representatives of eighty-one Communist Parties, from both socialist and capitalist countries alike, forgathered in Moscow.

In June 1969 only eight socialist countries out of fourteen were represented. In the case of the capitalist countries, several of the Parties represented only a fraction of their country's communist movement. This was notably so of Greece, only the fraction in exile in Moscow (which had approved the intervention in Czechoslovakia) being recognized, whereas Manolis Glezos and the whole of the internal Greek resistance were excluded from the Conference.[43]

43. The case of the Greek Communist Party is an extreme one. But since the invasion of Czechoslovakia the same method has been systematically applied by Brezhnev and the present leadership of the Communist Party of the Soviet Union. Basically they

The various schisms by which the Parties of Japan, India and Israel had been split meant that the delegations from those countries were less representative than they had been in 1960. The Indonesian Party, having been virtually wiped out, could not take part in the Conference.

In black Africa, Marxist parties are virtually non-existent.

In Latin America the inability of several of the Parties to shake off an imported model created in conditions wholly different from those prevalent in their respective countries, has led to a state of affairs in which large numbers of revolutionary forces are developing alongside and outside of the Parties, and sometimes even in opposition to them.

All in all there were over thirty Parties whose representation was limited, to say the least. And to this we would add that, of the three largest Parties from capitalist countries (Italy, France and Spain), one, that of Italy, refused to vote for the document, except for the first clause on solidarity in Vietnam, while another, the Spanish Com-

---

aim at eliminating at whatever cost—even that of reducing a Communist Party to a mere splinter group—all those militants, and especially their leaders, who not only condemned intervention in Czechoslovakia but, by endeavouring to discover the underlying reasons for it, disputed the concepts of the ruling apparatus in the Soviet Union.

It is significant that in Austria, at the time when the Communist Party Congress was in preparation, the Soviet leaders founded two periodicals with nominal editors only. One of these periodicals, *Berichte und Information*, published two special issues, the first directed against Ernst Fischer, a member of the Central Committee, the second against Franz Marek, a member of the Politburo. Both these men had demanded that light be thrown on the underlying causes of the disciplining of Czechoslovakia. The first periodical ceased publication as soon as it had attained the desired goal, namely the elimination of Fischer and Marek from the Party leadership. The second periodical, *Neue Politik*, continues its task of propaganda on behalf of neo-Stalinism.

munist Party, qualified its vote with numerous reservations. Other Parties, such as those of Great Britain and Belgium, registered their divergencies.

This could, indeed, be regarded as one of the most positive aspects of the Conference. In spite of the pressures exerted by the Soviet leaders in an attempt to prevent the airing of divergencies (notably on the subject of the Czechoslovak problem), there was genuine opposition, an opposition which stuck to its guns with such insistence that the Russians could no longer afford, as hitherto, to ignore the facts. This was a positive achievement because, far from signifying any dislocation of the movement, it meant that the 'monolithic' myth had been destroyed and that the time had come for real unity in the communist movement: An harmonious unity of Parties, each seeking for the specific model of socialism corresponding to its own social structures and national traditions, each exchanging experiences with the others on a basis of equality and complete autonomy of judgement and always prepared to rally to the common cause, above all to the struggle against imperialism.

Here we have a basis for true internationalism. For the international duty of each Communist Party does not now consist in constituting itself the instrument of propaganda and apologetics for an extraneous socialist model, but in making the demands of socialism felt, and felt deeply, inside its own country and in discovering the socialist model that corresponds to its country's own aspirations. This is how a Communist Party can contribute most fully to the common struggle of the international movement, as it could never do by giving its unquestioning approval to those who now determine the Soviet or Chinese policies.

The comparatively low number of Parties represented at the Moscow Conference, the unsatisfactory nature of their representation, and the divergencies which there found expression, were not the only manifestations of the crisis besetting the international communist movement. There was in addition the ideological weakness of the documents put up for vote.

Not one single decisive problem was resolved.

Not one single decisive problem was posed.

And the reason why not one single decisive problem was posed was because the analysis of the contradictions in the world today was altogether inadequate. For instance, the phrase, repeated parrot-fashion, that the contradictions in the capitalist world are becoming intensified has been applicable for at least fifty years. Yet it would be infinitely more pertinent to show that the contradictions in question are not quite the same as those in the nineteenth century, and that what is most significant today is not the fact that the working class is growing steadily poorer (an impoverishment that is, indeed, relative), but that, as the victim of the capitalist system's alienations, it is becoming steadily more alienated. This would help to explain why certain categories of non-manual workers who, as a consequence of the new scientific and technological revolution, are becoming increasingly integrated with the working class, are now painfully aware of that alienation and are turning radical not only because they are faced with growing exploitation but also because they refuse to become part of a system whose goals—or rather, whose absence of goals—they repudiate.

Again it is not enough to say that contradictions are becoming intensified only in the sense used by Marx when, a century ago, he said that capitalism contained within itself the limits of its own market. Since the depression of 1929-33 and the stopgap measures advocated by Keynes, involving the stimulation of monopolist State capitalism, the nature of both problems and contradictions has changed and, as we have shown in the case of the United

States, it is no longer possible to count on a crisis catastrophic enough to sweep away capitalism by the sheer exacerbation of its already intense contradictions.

Of all this there was no sign in the document.

Moreover, internal contradictions within the socialist camp were quite simply denied. And this at a time when, as if by chance, the 'ideological' argument between the U.S.S.R. and China had made way for a spate of border incidents and territorial disputes. At the very time, too, when the Russian occupation of Czechoslovakia had enforced, not only the abandonment of the 'line of January 1968', but also Party purges and compulsory self-criticism, with the threat of trials for anyone who sought an autochthonous model of socialism.

Therein lay the great weakness of the Conference and of its document. And the weakness consisted not so much in what was said as in what was left unsaid. In order to reach any kind of agreement it was necessary to delete from the text all reference to the vital problems posed by relations with China and Czechoslovakia.

This was to skirt the basic problem upon which the future of the movement depends, namely the question of the necessary and legitimate diversity of socialist models.

For instance, it is quite clear that Russia's intervention in Czechoslovakia implies her radical condemnation of the attempts by the Communist Parties of France and Italy to find a democratic road to socialism—a socialism in which there would be a plurality of parties, freedom of opinion and of the Press, and cooperation and dialogue with men who, though they may not have the same philosophy as ourselves, nevertheless share our desire for socialism.

Again, any analysis of the Chinese problem that was not merely polemical but also scientific would have required a fundamental reconsideration of the questions involved in the struggle for socialism in Asia, Africa and Latin America.

Rather than engage in a fundamental debate—a debate which could have given a tremendous impetus to the movement had it admitted a free confrontation such as would have questioned all dogmatisms, more especially those of Soviet and Chinese provenance—rather than engage in this debate, it was found better to exclude these questions, without any attempt to answer them. Thus the crucial problems of revolutionary strategy and socialist construction were simply bracketed out.

This inability, not only to face the fundamental problems which are at the root of the crisis in the international communist movement, but even so much as to recognize the existence of the crisis or its full extent and significance, has resulted in postponing once again that indispensable *aggiornamento* so hopefully presaged by the Twentieth Congress.[44]

What the present Soviet leaders were trying to do was to guide the Conference only along such lines as would serve to perpetuate their rule. This meant the suppression of all criticism of their invasion of Czechoslovakia and the reasons underlying it, as well as the transmogrification of the Moscow Conference into an anti-Chinese tribunal. Having confided to Husak the task of sweeping the Czechoslovak question under the carpet, Brezhnev himself set the tone where the attack on China was concerned, presenting that country as an anti-communist force. From this he went on to conclude that there was a need for a system of 'collective security in Asia' part of which, at least, would

44. It is significant that the *aggiornamento* of the Catholic Church, conjured up by the Second Vatican Council, has also undergone the same vicissitudes, the same attempts at restoration, the same repressive measures against those conscious of the historical necessity of the movement and its irreversible nature.

be directed against China. For a leading 'communist' this conclusion is not a little strange. For how is it possible to conceive of a coalition, whose composition would necessarily be hybrid, when the battle-field is Vietnam, when it's to Vietnam that China is giving her aid, when it's in Vietnam, the gateway to China, that the Americans are maintaining an army half a million strong? And what, it may be asked, has now become of proletarian internationalism or even of the basic concern for the victory of peace over imperialism?

Once again ideology comes to the rescue and justifies what is unjustifiable. The indubitable excesses of the present Chinese leaders are invoked as a pretext for declaring that China is no longer a socialist country and for vilifying her as Yugoslavia was vilified in Stalin's time, with the same old slogans—fascist clique, allies of imperialism, assassins, anti-communists, and so on and so forth.

On two previous occasions[45] we have attempted to analyse the Chinese problem; we have little to add to what we said then. Without touching on the roots of the problem, we shall therefore confine ourselves to a few notes on the Soviet leaders' campaign against China.

Aside from the excesses and mistakes of her leaders, in what way has China ceased to be socialist? Has the land been returned to the big landowners? No. The factories to the capitalists? No. And on the political plane what can the present Soviet leaders find to reproach her with? The immoderate use of violence? But compared with the massacres of Stalin's day, the violence unleashed by Mao's team appears insignificant. Yet no one would doubt that, even under Stalin, some form of socialism persisted—per-

45. Roger Garaudy, *Le Problème chinois* (Paperback edition, Seghers, Paris, 1967), and also, *Pour un modèle français du socialisme* (Gallimard, Paris, 1968), Part II, Ch. 1.

verted, perhaps, but socialism none the less—at least so far as the realization of its material circumstances was concerned. The argument against the Chinese is all the less valid in that under-development in China was even more serious than it had been in Russia, a situation that was considerably aggravated in 1960 when all Soviet aid abruptly ceased with the withdrawal of technologists and wholesale breaches of contract, the object being to cripple China's industrial progress and thus prepare the ground for effective ideological pressure. Can the argument then rest on China's use of force to back up her foreign policy? That force has seldom amounted to anything more than words, except in the case of the invasion of Indian territory in 1964 which was a serious mistake. But is it proper for those who have themselves invaded a socialist country to adopt a moralizing attitude here? Since the apocalyptic image which the present Soviet leaders paint of China is even more lurid than their picture of Czechoslovakia in 1968, might it not be pertinent to ask why they invaded the one country but not the other? Was it, perhaps, because the operation in the West seemed rather less hazardous? And no doubt this is also why Brezhnev has broken off diplomatic relations with Israel but not with the United States whose aggression is hardly less flagrant. There is small evidence here of political principles!

If Marxist analysis is applied to the reality of China as to the reality of the Soviet Union, it will be found that the problems cannot be posed in this way. It is as absurd to say that China has ceased to build socialism as to maintain, with the present Chinese leaders, that the Soviet Union has become a capitalist country.

A critical if objective examination of the Chinese model should help us not to forget, in the face of present perversions, the significance and greatness of the Chinese Revolution, in the same way that neither the Stalinist perversions nor those of the present Soviet leaders can make us forget the significance and greatness of the Russian October Revolution.

It is a curious fact that whereas proletarian internationalism is invoked to shield the Soviet leaders' policy from even the mildest criticism, the same internationalism can condone the worst of insults so far as China is concerned.

Now if a Marxist is to attain to a more objective judgement with regard to the Chinese problem, it would seem incumbent upon him to adhere to the guiding principles and fundamental coordinates of Marxist analysis.

1. The Chinese Revolution is essentially a peasant revolution. As early as 1920, Lenin had acknowledged that it was possible to pass directly[46] from a feudal régime to socialism without a transitional stage of capitalism and the latter's maturation. This implied, Lenin went on, a different conception of State and Party. In other words, he recognized *the legitimacy of a specific model*. Stalin and the Third International refused to adapt the revolutionary strategy in China to these original conditions but instead upheld the traditional thesis according to which it is the working class alone that can constitute socialism's spearhead. This strategy, by launching its attack on the strongholds of imperialism—the big towns of the littoral— brought about the massacre in Canton and Shanghai of the most resolute elements in the Chinese working class. But a strategy infinitely better adapted to Chinese conditions was evolved in 1927 by Mao Tse-tung—that of the 'country encircling the towns'—and proved so effective that it brought victory to the communists of China. Perhaps this may throw some light on the conflict with Liu Shao-chi who, after the foundation of the Chinese Communist Party, began to organize the urban masses, including both manual and non-manual workers. It would

46. Cf. R. Garaudy, *Le Problème chinois*, pp. 77-84.

eem that Liu had identified himself with the old Party apparatus just at a time when Mao Tse-tung, who was closer to the peasants, was entering the lists to combat the dangers of the new mandarinate in the shape of a bureaucratic organization of the Party.

Where they erred was in seeking to extrapolate this Chinese strategy on to other countries whose conditions were radically different; where they erred criminally was in maintaining that it had universal validity, thus bringing the countries of the Third World into opposition with the working class in the developed countries. The dogmatism and sectarianism of this ideological export policy has, in most countries, reduced pro-Chinese movements to the status of splinter-groups.

In China, however, the logic of this peasant revolution as applied to the construction of socialism rather than to the strategy of power seizure has meant that primitive accumulation could be realized by mobilizing man-power along lines completely unlike those of Western countries. This was so, firstly because the huge size of the country demanded the inversion of the classical model based upon industrialization followed by collectivization. Thus in China the change in social relations was employed to pave the way for industrialization. This process enabled them to circumvent two pitfalls—firstly a postponement of the country's self-sufficiency as regards food supplies, and secondly, a continuing if not prolonged exacerbation of the conflict between a few mammoth industrial combines and their agricultural hinterland. Decentralization was a vital precondition for China's metamorphosis. Agrarian collectivization, too, was carried out at less 'cost' in human terms than by Stalin's methods, being based on a much more discriminating analysis of rural class relations and social strata.

As regards industrialization, China had to start from much more rudimentary beginnings than did Russia in

1917, yet in spite of this and of bad mistakes resulting in wastage (e.g. the rural blast-furnaces of the Great Leap Forward), industrialization proceeded with great rapidity, its rate of growth being between 9 and 14 per cent. The first main targets for production were tools, agricultural machinery (more especially irrigation pumps), and fertilizers.

There are two prerequisites for this mode of development in a country where there is excessive demographic pressure; the first is primitive accumulation by means of voluntary human labour, the second is a mistrust of material incentives, for these would involve the risk of creating individualistic demands for luxury goods which in turn would upset the balance between the various sectors of production to the detriment both of basic and of collective needs.

2. The first consequence of such an orientation is to give pride of place to *subjective factors*, these being often overestimated. From this point of view the cultural revolution would appear to have set itself two main tasks:

Firstly, the attempt to prevent, by perhaps somewhat debatable means, the crystallization of bureaucracy within the Party apparatus so as to obviate the risk of a new mandarinate or of a new 'aristocracy of knowledge', an omniscient and more or less sclerotic dispenser 'from the outside' of socialism to the masses. But it was no simple matter to abolish within a few years the divine right of a culture which had lasted for several millennia. That is why we should think twice before uttering, from a distance, paternalistic strictures on an upheaval aimed at destroying medieval ways of thought, at extricating seven hundred million people from a rut two thousand years old, and mobilizing vast reserves of energy with which to banish once and for all the spell of mandarin or bourgeois authorities, as also that of foreign prototypes. To eliminate this danger Mao ran the risk of appealing to the masses over the head of the Party itself. It was an 'explosion' that bore a certain analogy to Khrushchev's procedure at the Twentieth Congress when, with scant support in the Politburo, and in somewhat dubious circumstances, he 'sprang the surprise' of Stalin's trial in order to produce what he believed to be an irreversible situation. Mao's appeal to the masses was an appeal to youth in a country where, out of seven hundred million inhabitants, one half—or three hundred and fifty millions—is under the age of twenty-one. The Party was not regarded as the only subjective factor in the revolution. The appeal to the historical initiative of the masses was in the Leninist tradition.

The second task assigned to the cultural revolution, a task of even vaster proportions, was to supplement the low level of the productive forces and the inadequacy of material conditions by developing the socialist consciousness. Undoubtedly this is in some ways a voluntarist, idealist excess which betrays the belief that it is possible to create a 'new man' before having realized the objective conditions necessary for that transformation. Yet here too we are closer to Marxism than was the mechanistic conception underlying Stalin's model, a model which postulated that, once the material bases of socialism had been created, a new man would necessarily emerge! If it were impossible to arouse the revolutionary spirit until all the objective conditions had been fulfilled, virtually no revolution could take place. The argument which the Russians have raised against the Chinese in this connection smacks unpleasantly of the objections levelled by Kautsky against Lenin.

It still remains, however, that 'the Chinese have changed' and that, in a country which had experienced thousands of years of stagnation and resignation, the Chinese Communist Party has largely succeeded in making hundreds of millions of men and women aware that it is in their power to change the world as it now is, along with its order and its hierarchies. True, there is the *Red Book* with its puerile dogmatism, but besides that there is televised education and an extremely up-to-date view, wholly in keeping with the demands of the new scientific and technological revolution, of education in general as an independent but crucial sector of the economy. As far back as January 1956 Chou En-lai said of this change, in his report on non-manual workers, that it was 'a revolution whose importance far exceeds that of the industrial revolution based upon steam and electricity'. That same year saw the emergence of a twelve-year plan for long-term research projects.

Since then, and in the course of a decade, China has simultaneously achieved her industrial revolution and her second scientific and technological revolution, the latter corresponding to the progress made in automation and in the exploitation of nuclear energy; striking testimony to this is provided by the manufacture of the H-bomb and of guided missiles. The scientific breakthrough was effected in many fields, from the manufacture of synthetic insulin and synthetic benzine to the separation of paraffin from petroleum by bacterial action.[47] Whatever the excesses that attended the realization of the cultural revolution and whatever the dogmatism that feeds on it, its actual principle cannot be condemned. For its virtue has not only consisted in getting rid of illiteracy and in disseminating a body of knowledge already extant if not actually canonized; it has also helped to inculcate in millions of men and women a vision of the world 'that transcends the self' and an unlimited confidence in man's power to change the world. Even though the cultural revolution may have been obscured by the conditions obtaining in China, some degree of critical objectivity will enable us to see it as a difficult but necessary stage in the realization of socialism in China.

47. In China as in the Soviet Union this breakthrough is limited to certain key sectors, not having become general through insufficient accumulation of capital in either country.

3. The Chinese Marxists have posed a third fundamental problem—that of *the plurality of the criteria for development*. By emphasizing, sometimes in a unilateral way, not only *quantitative* but also *qualitative* aspects, the Chinese communists have given urgency to the question of an alternative to societies of the American type, based on growth for growth's sake and on a religion of means. The glorification of a policy of frugality and asceticism is undoubtedly linked to a specific state of under-development, and its excesses have succeeded in giving an entirely false image of Marxist socialism—that of a collectivized misery which is the complete antithesis of Marx's thought. But the principle of seeking a new type of consumption, of forming new needs and a different model of civilization that is not based on individual comfort alone, has at least been stated and, if we shirk the problem, we shall be denying socialism the opportunity to reflect, as it must do, about its ends.

Yet unless it reflects deeply and critically, but at the same time objectively and scientifically, on the major problems posed by the Chinese revolution, there can be no serious dialogue with the Third World.

Now it is tragically evident that in the narrow-minded and virulent campaign conducted by the Soviet leaders against China not one of the three fundamental problems has ever been broached: the problem of the necessary diversity of models, the problem of the role and the limitations of the subjective factor in revolution and the problem of the plurality of criteria for development.

If these problems are tackled directly, not only does the dialogue with the Third World become possible, but also the necessary critical objectivity in regard to the historical course described by the countries of Europe since the Renaissance. And this will entail a revision of all our traditional conceptions of man's relations with nature, with society, with his gods and with the future.

Only then can we embark on a valid critique of the

Chinese model and of the theoretical and practical conduct of the present Chinese leaders.

Strange though it may seem, when the Czechoslovak communists[48] were striving to work out a socialist model in keeping with the new scientific and technological revolution in a highly developed country, they were posing the same problems to the communist movement—if in different circumstances and from a different viewpoint—as have now been posed by the Chinese communists: the problems, that is, of the diversity of models, as also of the Party's role and, more generally, of the subjective factor in revolution; finally, the problem of the plurality of criteria for development, namely that which arises out of the creation of a specifically socialist alternative to the model of civilization presented by the 'consumer societies' of capitalism.

That is why the elimination of the problems relating to China and Czechoslovakia, in accordance with the Soviet leaders' will, meant that the Moscow Conference inevitably failed to tackle any of the communist movement's crucial problems.

The Soviet leaders either refuse to see or choose to ignore the deep contradictions in the socialist world, attributing all the difficulties of the movement to 'imperialist conspiracy' or to 'ideological subversion'.

There can be no doubt whatever that there have been and still are in Czechoslovakia counter-revolutionary forces which exploit the trend towards democracy with a view, not to the improvement of socialism, but to its destruction. Nor can there be any doubt that extraneous elements and even agents of foreign imperialism are fanning the flames and exploiting the situation. But to leave it at that is to shirk the problem since this prohibits any attempt to under-

48. R. Garaudy, *Prague ou la Liberté en sursis* (Fayard, Paris, 1968), and *Pour un modèle français du socialisme*, Part II, Ch. III.

stand how it is that the enemies of socialism are still able to elicit some response. And whereas the situation that gave rise to the cleavage between Party and people—a situation for which Novotny and his Russian advisers were responsible—went unquestioned, those who, under extremely difficult circumstances, had attempted to retrieve that situation, namely Dubcek and his companions, were forced by the Stalinists into self-accusations and found themselves threatened with the prospect of trial.

Now when in August 1969, a year after the invasion, the nationwide feeling of unrest was attributed to some tens of hundreds of young people, or again to foreign *agents provocateurs*, this was clearly an attempt to conceal the main cause which was in fact the nation's unanimous rejection of the occupation.

To contend that a few louts were responsible for the disorders is to argue like the journalists who accompanied Rockefeller on his travels through Latin America and who dismissed the protest of a whole continent against the exploitation and oppression of Yankee imperialism by attributing the demonstrations he encountered there to a few student splinter groups ostensibly following him round from one capital to another.

Time was in France when every strike was attributed by the employers, the government and the organs of their Press to a 'clandestine *chef d'orchestre*', an agitator in the pay of Moscow! They, too, were looking for 'ideological subversion' so that they could turn a blind eye to the deep social contradictions which give rise to great autochthonous labour movements.

Now Lenin, in 1919, at a time when things were most difficult, did not hesitate to challenge the rest of the world to a free exchange of propaganda pamphlets. Can a country's leaders who, for fifty years, have had a monopoly of all the communication media, now really be so much on the defensive that, having formed three entire generations, they still fear 'ideological subversion' by the capitalist world?

Though the ill is deep-seated, there is some reason for hope.

To take objective reasons first. The development of the economic reform cannot be interrupted or even fettered for very long without creating grave difficulties in the supply situation and perhaps even jeopardizing the country's defence. It is a path that must be followed willy-nilly, and moreover, as we have already seen, one of the inherent factors in that reform is the democratization of social activities generally, more especially in the political and cultural fields. Without it the reform would not be viable.

There is also a certain amount of pressure from the outside world. The 'bureaucratic-military complex' now carries almost as much weight in the U.S.S.R. as does the military-industrial complex in the United States,[49] its influence having made itself particularly felt in the political role played by Marshal Gretzhko in the Czechoslovak affair. This complex cannot continue indefinitely to impose upon neighbouring socialist countries a socialist model and structures that can only be maintained by police and military coercion. There can be no doubt that some of the Soviet leaders themselves are alive to the danger of potential explosions, even in countries other than Czechoslovakia, and are considering the possibility of alternative, non-coercive solutions and methods.

If the Soviet Union wishes in future to avoid reverses such as it has already suffered in the field of cybernetics and lunar exploration, it must meet the growing demand inherent in the development of the new scientific and technological revolution: the demand for democracy at every

49. There is no real comparison, for in the United States the military-industrial complex is both an economic and a political phenomenon, whereas in the U.S.S.R. the bureaucratic-military complex is a predominantly political phenomenon.

level, from production to scientific research—a question we have already discussed earlier in this work.

Pressure by fraternal Communist Parties, like that exerted at the Moscow Conference by the delegates from Spain and Italy, could give a powerful impetus to this recovery.

In the Soviet Union itself, and in spite of the strict censorship on news, protest, especially among scientists of the first rank such as those who created the H-bomb or the missiles, carries a great deal of weight which could cause the bureaucratic-military complex to beat a retreat.

It is true, however, that the structure of the system itself does not permit of any correction or any change of political orientation by normal democratic means. This can only happen either as the result of an explosion, such as took place at the Twentieth Party Congress, or through a 'palace revolution' of the kind that brought about the eviction of Khrushchev.

Thus it is not impossible that the present leading caucus might one day be swept aside, making way for a renewal which would restore to the October Revolution its true countenance and its dynamic force.

There is an increasingly perceptible contradiction between the political and ideological superstructures which constrict development on the one hand and, on the other, the new structures of the Soviet economy and the inner logic of the economic reform which demands a true socialist democracy. What will be the outcome? Either the preservation of the bureaucratic-military complex which will result in reactionary neo-Bonapartism and the dictatorship of the army. Or else a profound democratic renewal that will restore the true face of socialism—the liberation, that is, of labour and of man from all forms of alienation.

# 4 Alternative Models of Socialism

Where the elaboration of a socialist model is concerned, the major problem today is presented by the new scientific and technological revolution. How can we overcome the potential contradiction between the scientific ordering of production and the autonomy of the worker?

This is a contradiction which, as we have seen in connection with the United States, is insurmountable in a capitalist régime: the solution requires a radical change in the relations of production. So long as technocracy is largely controlled and directed by private ownership of the means of production—by big monopolies for example —there will be osmosis between the imperative of profit and the imperative of growth for growth's sake; the alienation of the workers and of society as a whole will continue to grow.

In order to begin to reduce this alienation it will first be necessary to put an end to private ownership of the means of production whose abolition is the starting point for the construction of socialism. While this is a necessary precondition it is not wholly adequate, as our analysis of the Soviet model has shown.

The Soviet socialist model is characterized by the identification of collective ownership of the means of production with State ownership. But it is by no means axiomatic that the revolutionary role of the proletarian State should be transformed into an administrative one.

Socialist revolution necessarily implies the seizure of political power by the working class and its allies for the specific purpose of bringing about a radical change in the relations of production and their expression in law—the right of ownership.

The revolutionary function of the new class State, where the problem of property is concerned, consists not only in the abolition of private ownership of the means of production and the substitution of a social ownership which is indivisible and inalienable, but also in the laying down of 'rules of the game' to frustrate a return to private ownership whether by individuals or by groups whose members might employ and exploit the wage-earners or else turn themselves into private shareholders.

If the State in its economic role goes beyond this transformation of the relations of production and beyond the laying down of 'rules of the game', its revolutionary function turns into an administrative one. In the early stages of the revolution the State may be led to adopt the latter function for historical reasons—a shortage both of goods and of cadres, and also the need for a war economy and extreme concentration of power and resources to combat counter-revolutionary activities.

But if this administrative function, while both legitimate and necessary during the period of 'War Communism', continues beyond that period, State ownership will diverge increasingly from the early form of social ownership of the means of production which it may have assumed during the assault phase of the revolution.

The State is not society. It is the instrument for repression and domination by one class. But even when it is the instrument for domination and repression by the working class it still remains distinct from society as a whole and even from the working class as a whole. We have already recalled Lenin's assessment of this phenomenon made as early as 1919 and 1920: '. . . our is a workers' State *with a bureaucratic twist* to it . . . the Soviets, which by virtue of their programme are organs of government *by the working people*, are in fact organs of government *for the working people* by an advanced section of the proletariat, but not by the working people as a whole . . . we, for our part, must use these workers' organisations to protect the workers from their State . . .'[1]

Indeed the State is not an abstraction but rather the embodiment of a group of people: 'Bureaucracy', wrote Marx, 'possesses the substance of the State . . . the State becomes its property.'[2]

In a socialist model where social ownership is permanently identified with State ownership, administration becomes the monopoly, speciality and profession of one particular social group.

This group's main prerogatives are:

1. Monopoly of the administration of State property,
2. As a corollary of 1, monopoly of political decision through the laying down of objectives and programmes,
3. Monopoly in the use of newly created values, of surplus-value.

The two fundamental reasons why this bureaucracy does not constitute a social class are firstly that it is merely the administrator, not the owner, of the means of production, and secondly that these administrative powers are not, like property, hereditary.

The fact still remains that this identification of social property with State property in a centralized bureaucratic State does not permit a satisfactory solution to the problem of adapting to the new scientific and technological revolution which, as we have seen, demands participation on the widest scale as well as responsibility and creative initiative on the part of all. Nor does it permit a satisfactory solution to the problem of disalienation—socialism's main objective—since the worker in such a system

1. See above Ch. 3, pp. 81, 82.
2. Karl Marx, 'Critique of Hegel's Philosophy of Right' in *Early Writings* (C. A. Watts, London, 1963).

is once again turned into a wage-earner, albeit as a State, and not a private, employee.

The elaboration of a different model requires from the start the clear knowledge that State property is only one form among others of social property. To achieve this knowledge it is necessary to recall the several constituents of the concept of property and the concept of State.

Marx distinguished between property as an appropriation of nature by man's labour which transforms it, and property, alienated in every class society, where the determination of the goals and of the fruits of labour is the privilege and monopoly of the owner of the means of production.[3]

Marx's analysis enables us to assign a precise content to the classical distinctions used in law concerning the ownership of the means of production: *usus, fructus, abusus.*

*Usus* is primarily the power to lay down the goals of production, either for profit, for social or individual needs, or for any other purpose. Next it denotes the power to determine the organization, the methods, the rate of work, and to ensure the technological administration of the undertaking.

*Fructus* is the disposal of the fruits of labour, in other words the appropriation of surplus-value and control over its use and distribution—immediate consumption, investment, etc.

*Abusus* is the right to 'dispose as master' of the object possessed, to use it or abuse it, the right, where a means of production is concerned, to destroy it, sell it or convert it entirely into consumer goods.

The ownership of this property may be vested in a

3. This analysis was outlined by Marx in his *Economic and Philosophical Manuscripts of 1844* and taken up again in a more exact form in *Capital.*

single individual, in a group, in the State (either in the guise of State capitalism or of State socialism), or in a society's workers as a whole. It may also exist in mixed form, as for example the 'workers' control' introduced by Lenin, which, while leaving the ownership of certain means of production to the proprietors, began by excluding *abusus*, that is the destruction of the means of production in the shape of waste or sabotage, and went on to impose controls on *usus* and *fructus*. With regard to *usus* this meant that checks were carried out on the quantity of merchandise produced, production being directed towards the satisfaction of the most pressing needs. It also meant the supervision of technical management lest the latter should fail to produce the supplies needed or to respect working conditions. Lastly, controls were imposed on *fructus*, through taxation designed to limit profits.

As to the State, if its revolutionary function is 'exhausted' in the process of abolishing private property rights and laying down 'rules of the game' to prevent their reinstatement (whether in individual or collective form), it does not necessarily follow that spontaneity should be allowed free play in production and in economic life generally. By renouncing the role of universal administrator, the revolutionary State may largely assign the right of ownership and of the disposal of surplus-value to the workers themselves; in this way it may leave to other factors of social integration—factors which are neither administrative nor authoritarian—the responsibility for orientating production according to need and for setting up forms of management which will ensure maximum productivity through the maximum participation of workers in any given management.

What then are the other characteristics of this 'model', aside from the four criteria of property defined above?

The orientation of production, contrary to capitalist practice, becomes a function not of profit but of the needs of society, and this distinguishes all forms of socialism. But contrary to practice in the statist, centralist (Soviet) model, these needs will not be determined from 'above' through central directives by the State and Party but by the action of the *market* and of the demands which this discloses. If we remember that what takes place in this market is a confrontation between socialist rather than private undertakings it will be clear that such a market economy is not a capitalist economy. On the other hand it is true that the individual needs which exert their pressure there are influenced, if not determined, by the level of the productive forces, by antecedent hardships, by external models, etc. But to escape that would entail a turning towards subjectivism and idealism, towards a belief in the magic properties of decisions 'from above' made by omniscient leaders who have set themselves in the workers' stead as the infallible interpreters of their needs. It would further entail a belief in the magic properties of a 'morality' divorced from its material context. Marx's axiom about right is indeed applicable to all social rules: 'Right can never be higher than the economic structure of society and the cultural development thereby determined.'[4]

Where property is concerned the Yugoslav Constitution of 1963 (Basic Principles, Section II) proclaims that the inviolable basis of the system is social ownership of the means of production aimed at the abolition of 'man's alienation from the means of production and other conditions of labour'.

In defining the characteristics of self-management, Section III contains the words: 'Since no one has the right of ownership over socially-owned means of production, nobody—neither socio-political communities nor individual working-men—may appropriate on any legal basis the product of social labour, or manage and dispose of socially-

4. Karl Marx, *A Critique of the Gotha Programme* (Lawrence & Wishart, London, 1941), p. 14.

owned means of production, or arbitrarily determine the terms of their distribution.

'Man's labour is the only ground for the appropriation of the product of social labour and the basis for the management of social resources.'

Thus the Constitution, in order to eliminate any form of alienation from the conditions and product of labour, withholds the right of any person or group to possess a monopoly of social property. For example the factories do not belong either to the State or to the workers' collectives but are administered by the latter in the name and interest of society as a whole.

In matters of technological administration today's technocrats, engineers, technologists and experts play a necessarily important role. But this is an inevitable consequence of the increasingly scientific organization of production. The only problem is to know who supervises these technocrats and technologists, and in accordance with what aims and criteria. Up to the present the different forms of society now in existence have provided what amounts to three different answers to these questions:

in the capitalist countries, control and direction are ultimately exercised by the owners of the means of production, i.e. the big monopolies;

in socialist countries of the centralist statist type, by the ruling group in the Party and State;

in socialist countries seeking a model based on 'self-management', by the workers' collectives.

With regard to the last system the objection has been raised that in Yugoslavia the central workers' council in large undertakings includes a considerable number of experts and engineers. This is indisputable. But it should be stressed, firstly, that they have been *elected* to this council by the workers themselves; secondly, that they are obliged to keep the workers as a whole *informed* and to secure their agreement to each important decision by convincing them of its rightness (though here the workers' collective may demand different, indeed contradictory, information from experts independent of the undertaking); and finally that these discussions, combined with the flow of information, represent a means of permanent education which raises the technological and cultural level of everyone concerned and thus permits not only an increasing measure of participation but also the access of all to managerial functions.

It would, however, be Utopian to seek by artificial means to go beyond the existing level of skills and impose *'ouvriériste'* norms which, under pretext of combating technocracy, would be prejudicial to the progress both of men and of production and hence prejudicial to the workers as a whole.

The fact is that before any election there is a discussion of the criteria which should govern the choice of candidates having regard to the orientation of the undertaking, and further the list of candidates is decided at a general meeting of the workers.

In every socialist country the *fructus*, which is essentially the same as *surplus-value*, ceases to be appropriated by the private owner of the means of production. But it may be wholly at the disposal of a centralized State which will be the sole arbiter of the portion to be set aside for investment and of the nature of that investment as also of the portion to be set aside for consumption. Alternatively the State will only appropriate a greater or lesser amount of the surplus-value in order to finance public expenditure (defence, major works, etc.) while allowing the different undertakings and work units to allocate the balance of this surplus-value as they see fit. In the case of Yugoslavia the tendency over the past twenty years has been to allow the undertakings to retain a growing share of the surplus-value. From the time of writing up to 1970, the State's share will be 30 per cent and that of the undertaking 62 per cent, the latter being empowered to decide how much of its portion to allocate to investment and how much to consumption.

We shall presently examine the actual functioning of the system of which we have just sketched the abstract model. But before beginning this investigation, one final word is needed to stress the historical importance of the experiment although it has hitherto only been carried out in a small country, namely Yugoslavia. Even in socialist countries where the statist, centralized model has been retained, the demands of development have led to economic reforms all of which (and this includes the Soviet Union) are moving in the direction of the 'model' towards which Yugoslavia has been tending since 1950. This is particularly evident in the growing role conceded to the market and in the recognition that undertakings should have a degree of autonomy. Yugoslavia's aspirations to a new model are not, therefore, an accident of history; rather they express an essential aspect of the inward logic of a socialist society's development.

It may appear paradoxical that several of the features of a socialist model capable of responding to the demands of the new scientific and technological revolution should have found their first expression in a small country, more especially one handicapped from the outset by acute underdevelopment.

How is this paradox to be explained?

In 1945, after four years of partisan warfare, Yugoslavia was virtually unique among European countries in having, by her own force of arms, liberated herself almost entirely from Nazi occupation before the arrival of Allied troops. The socialist system instituted by the Yugoslav communists immediately after the cessation of hostilities tended to imitate the centralist Soviet model. Indeed rigorous centralization was demanded by the exigencies of war followed by reconstruction and the first stages in the struggle against under-development—circumstances, that is, analogous to those obtaining in Russia in 1917.

After 1948 bureaucratic distortions threatened the revolution. In her turn Yugoslavia was learning things the hard way—that socialism cannot be reduced to a formula for the realization of primitive accumulation without losing its human significance. The socialization of production is essential if capitalist exploitation is to be abolished. But hypertrophy of the State apparatus and the latter's centralized, bureaucratic, authoritarian structure are responsible for the continued alienation of the working class, even after the State has abolished capitalist exploitation. This is contrary to the very principle of socialism, a principle which does not simply imply a reorganization of the relations of production but also, and in consequence of these new relations, a liberation of the workers from all forms of alienation, so permitting the full flowering of man and of all men which is the ultimate goal of socialism.

At the start this contradiction was obscured, firstly by the immediate and urgent tasks of restoring the economy and of primitive accumulation, and secondly by the prestige of the model elaborated by the Soviet Union which, as the first to breach the capitalist system in October 1917 and the first to offer a genuine alternative to capitalist rule, was held to represent the only possible form of socialism.

Yugoslavia's excommunication by Stalin and the 'Cominform'[5] in 1948 and the sanctions that were instantly applied to compel her, by paralysing her economy, to adopt the official ideology were disastrous for the country. For more than a year she was threatened by famine which

5. The Cominform was the information committee of the Communist Parties and was in fact, a reconstitution of the Comintern, in other words the Communist International, in an ostensibly less rigid form. During the Second World War the Comintern had been dissolved in order to allow the various Communist Parties greater autonomy in the formulation of their national policy.

forced her, for the sake of survival, to seek help from the capitalist countries.

Yet this terrible crisis was not without its positive side: an attack of such dimensions from the socialist camp, in conformity with the line laid down by Stalin, led to the lifting of an ideological taboo. An inquiry into the causes of the intervention induced the Yugoslav communists—as it induced other communists, twenty years later, after the intervention in Czechoslovakia—to ask themselves whether the origin of so flagrant a violation of the officially proclaimed principles of proletarian internationalism and of each Party's autonomy was not a bureaucratic, dogmatic and authoritarian perversion of the socialist system such as had evolved in the Soviet Union after Lenin's death.

The sheer brutality of the blow cleared the way for a critical analysis of the Soviet model. Inevitably there were polemical excesses (readily understandable at a time when Cominform resolutions were proclaiming, as in 1949 for example: 'The Yugoslav Communist Party is in the hands of spies and assassins', and were calling on the peoples of Yugoslavia to rise up against the rule of Party and State). Yet in the midst of all this Yugoslavia experienced a revival of Marxist scholarship; though not entirely without serious shortcomings, it aroused a new interest in the works of Marx, Engels and Lenin as sources of theoretical standards against which to measure Soviet practice and to reassess her own.

In Yugoslavia this reappraisal was made easier by the fact that since the bureaucratic apparatus had then not been in existence for more than a few years, its hold on the country was less than that maintained in the Soviet Union by the Stalinist system which had been in operation for a quarter of a century. Moreover in Yugoslavia, home of Europe's most significant partisan movement, the vitality of the 'partisan spirit'—a combination of discipline and initiative—had created a situation in which popular demand at substructure level for a share in decision-making was exceptionally strong.

It cannot be denied that in the course of this profound reappraisal, tendencies came to light that were egalitarian to the point of anarchy and certain theoreticians even ventured, in a libertarian, Proudhonian spirit, to extol immoderately the virtues of untrammelled spontaneity.

But the conclusion which ultimately emerged from all this, to be adopted by the leaders of the Yugoslav Communist Party as the general line, was to return to the teachings of Lenin, bypassing the image of Leninism as codified by Stalin.

They recalled how Lenin had always been careful to draw a distinction between questions relating to principle and provisional measures dictated by a state of war, emergency or siege.

The basic texts on 'workers' control' were systematically studied. Once again the voice of Lenin was heard, speaking to the Third Congress of the Soviets in January 1918 on the building of the new socialist economy: 'In introducing workers' control, we knew that it would take much time before it spread to the whole of Russia but we wanted to show that we recognize only one road—changes from below; we wanted the workers themselves, from below, to draw up the new, basic economic principles . . . We know perfectly well the difficulties that confront us in this work; but we assert that only those who set to work to carry out this task relying on the experience and the instinct of the working people are socialists in deed. The people will commit many mistakes . . . The workers and peasants have not yet sufficient confidence in their own strength; age-old tradition has made them far too used to waiting for orders from above . . . The intelligence of tens of millions of creators provides something infinitely higher than expectations, however vast and genial these may be.'[6]

6. Lenin, *Works*, Vol. 26, pp. 467 et seq.

'We must offer the popular masses complete freedom to create.'[7]

'Socialism is not the result of decrees that come from above. Administrative and bureaucratic automatism is foreign to its nature; living, creative socialism is the work of the popular masses themselves.'[8]

'Workers' control shall be exercised by all the workers and office employees of an enterprise, either directly, if the enterprise is small enough to permit it, or through their elected representatives, who shall be elected *immediately* at general meetings . . .'[9]

Such were the points of departure for the Yugoslav communists when pondering the elaboration of a socialist model based on the maximum participation of the workers in the making of decisions. This they described as a model based on self-management in contrast to one based on centralism.

Socialism based on self-management, as the Yugoslav communists themselves are ready to point out, is not a *fait accompli*. Its full realization is hampered by a number of obstacles, some objective—in particular the inherited burden of under-development—others subjective, more especially the ceaseless struggle against libertarian, disruptive tendencies, against the survival of a bureaucratic, authoritarian mentality and against nostalgia for the expediency of a Stalin-type régime.

But after twenty years the policy still obtains, inspiring the theoretical work as well as the essential practical measures.

Taking as their point of departure an analysis of the essence of Stalinism, the Yugoslav communists set about the transformation of the socialist model by instituting a series of measures designed to *contain and reverse the tendency towards the State control of society*, a tendency which, as Lenin had shown, leads to the substitution of the

7. Ibid.        8. Ibid.
9. Lenin, 'Our Revolution', *Works*, Vol. 26, p. 264.

Party and State for the working class and to the construction of socialism *for*, but not *by* the working class.

Their first step in this direction was taken at the beginning of 1950 when they checked the growth of the State apparatus by abolishing some 100,000 government posts.

The second step, which set in motion an irreversible process, dispelled the confusion over social property and State property; under the law of 27 June 1950 the management of the factories was turned over to the workers.

This marked the 'turning-point' on the road to self-management.

Three principal ideas were to govern all the subsequent evolution of the system:

1. State property must become social property administered not by one single, ostensibly omniscient centre but by the entire body of direct producers and workers. Thus there was a move from the conception of centralized planning to a conception that placed an increasing measure of confidence in the initiative of the substructure.

2. This new form was to spread from the economy to social relations in general. The 'withering away' of the State foreseen by Marx and Engels could not be adjourned indefinitely, for without it the cells in the substructure of society, deprived of a life of their own, would be no more than the executive instruments of the omnipotent centre whence all directives came. This and every other field was to see the beginning of the *great inversion* whereby the centralized, bureaucratic State is replaced by a system of autonomy in which millions of men make the decisions that are vital to their destiny.

3. The Party must distance itself from the State apparatus so as to avoid becoming an organ of the executive and also to ensure that it is the true expression of the whole

*153*

class, the class's theoretical consciousness. For the Party's primary mission is not to issue directives but to stimulate and coordinate initiatives.

A fortunate combination of circumstances—the survival of the partisan spirit, the shock of the Stalinist attack which galvanized the will to independence of the whole people, the comparatively recent 'installation' of the State and Party apparatus as a privileged caste—helped to reduce the resistance of the bureaucratic machine when it came to breaking the latter's monopoly, and obviated the need for a Chinese style 'cultural revolution' with all its attendant dangers.

But a 'long march', still far from being concluded, was necessary before the factories could be managed effectively by the workers, the communes by the citizens, the universities by the teachers and students, the insurance funds by the insured, and so on. Nor could the march be easy since the circumstances most favourable to the full realization of a socialist model based on self-administration are those in which the productive forces give full play to the effects of the cybernetic revolution and where the 'collective labourer' (in the indivisible unity of its manual and non-manual work) is able to control production in a conscious and autonomous fashion.

In Yugoslavia these two conditions had still not been met in 1969—even less so in 1950. It has therefore been found necessary, as Lenin found it necessary in his day, to stand a theoretical schema on its head. In the same way that Lenin had not hesitated to invert the 'ideal' order of economic maturity followed by the seizure of political power and instead had first changed social and political relations, before going on to promote the development of the productive forces and economic maturation,[10] so the Yugoslav communists, with a material base that was still weak, put their faith in a move towards autonomy by the

10. See beginning of Ch. 3.

manual and non-manual workers who thus learned to play an increasingly effective part in decision-making.

The first prerequisite for the change was the transition from State ownership—in itself a cause of the proliferation of the bureaucratic caste—to social ownership by the workers as a whole. For a socialist democracy cannot exist when the working class formally in power is deprived of the principal right of every governing class, namely the right to dispose of the surplus-value of social labour.

If this right remains the monopoly of a centralized bureaucratic machine the condition of the working class as a whole will continue to be one of dependence and alienation. All institutions, even those ostensibly the most democratic, will then, as before under bourgeois democracy, resume a 'formal' character. Thus the Stalinist Constitution of 1936, for instance, which formulated admirable principles, was promulgated when the period of trials, purges and massacres was at its worst. Or again, it was at the time when the 1969 Moscow Conference was solemnly recalling the principles of non-intervention and the autonomy of each Party, that in Czechoslovakia a model alien to her requirements and contrary to the wishes of her people and Party was imposed in the name of a centralized and authoritarian ideology which ended up by identifying all democratic change with the disintegration of socialism.

In accordance with the principle of self-management the producer in Yugoslavia possesses all the rights. According to Article 10 of the Constitution, it is for him to decide 'as directly as possible' not only the conditions of labour but also the allocation of income or surplus-value.

As in Lenin's plan for workers' control, the workers' councils in the small factories (those employing up to thirty people) comprise the entire labour force. In the large undertakings the councils consist of members elected by all the employees each of whom has the right to attend committee meetings. No one may be elected to the council twice running, thus ensuring maximum participation by means of a system of rotation.

The workers themselves decide their production policy and thereby become the effective heirs to the actual rights pertaining to owners of the means of production. The sole 'rule of the game' is that they may not destroy the means of production (unless it be to replace it with a better one) and that they may not, as a group, exploit other workers—anyone joining an undertaking enjoys all the rights of those already employed there.

Subject to these two reservations the workers' collective decides on the quality, quantity and kind of product, and also, once its obligations to society as a whole have been fulfilled, on the distribution of profits (investment, rates of pay, etc.).

The condition of the workers depends not on norms set by those 'above' but on the product's success in the market.

Thus it is possible to avoid the subjectivism of direction from above without presuming to escape from objective economic laws. While the capitalist category of profit no longer exists under socialism by virtue of the fact that social ownership has replaced private ownership of the means of production, the law of value continues to operate. This is a fact Stalin himself was compelled to admit five years after the turning-point in Yugoslavia. At the existing level of development of the productive forces it is not possible to dismiss either the market's regulatory role or the law of value based on the existence of that market. If, in the centralized planning of requirements, resources and production, the laws of the market are disregarded, the lack of balance between requirements and production will inevitably manifest itself in gross inconsistencies such as unsold stocks or, conversely, a disappearance of goods from the market resulting in fraud and black-market operations.

The restoration of a market economy is not an end in itself. It even contains grave dangers, the first being that all human values will become commercialized, but it is an inevitable stage on the way to a certain level of development of the productive forces. So true is this that all the socialist countries, beginning with the U.S.S.R., have been compelled to admit these facts a few years after Yugoslavia, and to steer their economic reforms in a similar direction.

A market economy cannot be abolished by decree: it will only disappear when bulk consumer goods are so plentiful that they no longer possess 'value'.

So efficient is the system that between 1960 and 1966 the increase in the gross national product *per capita* was greater in Yugoslavia (along with Romania) than in any other socialist country, the U.S.S.R. included.[11] When it comes to a comparison with the capitalist countries we should note that the raising of labour productivity in agriculture as well as in industry has been such that Yugoslavia is the first socialist country to be in the process of effecting—though admittedly not without difficulty —the convertibility of her currency *vis-à-vis* the capitalist countries.

These achievements make it easier to reply to certain objections raised *a priori* and without a concrete study of the system.

1. How can self-management work in very large nationwide undertakings such as the railways, post office and electricity service which demand a high level of technological knowledge in those who control them?

First of all it is obvious that in undertakings like these self-management can only function indirectly, that is through a representative system, since a meeting of the entire labour collective is wholly impracticable.

The problem of democratic administration has been solved by the creation of a number of distinct levels of de-

11. *Yearbook of National Accounts Statistics*, United Nations, 1967.

cision. In the case of the railways, for example, four levels have been established for the workers' councils (all of whose members are elected by the railwaymen). At the top level decisions are made affecting technical problems such as timetables and coordination with other European railway systems. Investment and accumulation, on the other hand, are dealt with at the next level, along with fares, extensions to the system, and research, all of which are linked with the country's long-term development. Neither the Government, nor the Republics, nor the Federations are represented on this body. In the Economic Chamber, on the other hand, the railwaymen's representatives may confront more general interests. The Transport Commission of this Assembly, however, does not make decisions but instead lays down guidelines. There is no denying that the system sometimes fails to obviate contradictions and conflicts of interest as, for instance, when regional requirements happen to compete, yet we ought to regard it as significant that, both here and generally in all other sectors, self-management does not slow down development. For example the newly constructed lines from Sarajevo to Ploce and from Belgrade to Bar have not shown an immediate profit because they pass through areas that remain largely under-developed. But their very existence makes possible the development of these areas at some future date which in turn will help to raise the profitability of the railways. That these and similar problems should have met with a positive response when put to the railwaymen is proof that their decisions are not influenced merely by their immediate interests; in consenting to set aside a portion of the revenue for the modernization of equipment they were concerned more with their long-term prospects than with an early wage increase. Further proof is provided by the fact that on the occasion of a loan being floated for the purpose of modernizing railway equipment, ninety per cent was subscribed by the railwaymen. Such an action would be inconceivable in any régime where there was no apparent economic relationship between present sacrifice and future gain.

2. How is self-management effected in enterprises which do not show an immediate return—universities for example?

Here again the State as such is not represented. The operative body is the 'educational community' which, within the framework of the Republics, consists of representatives of the workers' councils, the social services, the teachers, and the students.

This community works out long-term plans for the university's development and attends to problems of finance. The necessary financial support is provided by the large undertakings since these depend on the universities for the cadres they require. In addition help is provided by the State which makes available, on average, grants corresponding to between thirty-five and fifty per cent of the cost of basic research. It does not, however, lay down a norm for the contribution made by undertakings.

The Council of Culture and Education of the Federal Assembly on the other hand, puts forward general syllabuses, standards for the recruitment of teachers, and rules for the awarding of degrees, but in the form of guidelines rather than directives.

The university councils (consisting of the teachers and of representatives elected by the students) draw up the university statutes, decide on plans and syllabuses, dispose of the funds allocated to the university and settle the problems of the cadres, all this being done on an autonomous basis.

Here again it would be foolish to play down the difficulties—bureaucratic opposition from the older State organizations as well as unequal treatment of the teachers with its corollary of competition (which does not exclude

emulation) between universities. There is, too, a tendency
to favour the natural sciences as being more likely to show
a quick return than the humanities. (But what régime,
whether it be the United States, the Soviet Union or for
that matter, France, is immune from this temptation?)

3. A third objection to the system of self-management
turns on the difficulty of administering enterprises which,
in the present state of science and technology, require high
skills. This is a very real problem. But neither a simplistic
view of self-management, nor Proudhonian theories, nor
*a priori* judgements will help here. What is needed is
direct reference to Yugoslavia's concrete experiment from
which it will be found that the cadres, usually those most
highly qualified, play a major role in compiling the 'dos-
siers' required for decision-making. The relative importance of the part played by the engineers and technologists
or by the economist responsible for the project will vary
according to whether the workers' council is discussing,
say, production plans, the renewal of plant and equipment,
or the question of outlets. The management of a large
undertaking represents a complex scientific problem. Each
individual brings to the meeting of the workers' council
his own particular abilities and his own particular understanding of that problem.

It would be pure demagogy to suggest that all of them
are capable of answering every question. What really
matters is that they should all be made aware by the
specialists of the various choices available; that they
should have the opportunity of discussing them and of re-
questing information (which may well be contradictory)
from experts independent of the undertaking; that they
should be enabled to form an opinion on the general course
to be adopted, on working conditions and on wages. It
should be added that the cadres who submit future projects are answerable to the whole body of the workers for

the execution as also for the success or failure of their schemes.

Here then are the premises of an authentic social democracy even if its actual manner of progression is not always smooth—a consequence, primarily of under-development and initial retardation.

4. It has sometimes been asked whether the workers, by being entitled to dispose freely of the surplus-value created (the fundamental principle, that is, of self-management), do not tend to absorb it in wages to the detriment of growth and investment. Such would probably be the case in a capitalist or in a socialist, centralized bureaucratic system where there is no direct economic link between voluntary effort and the ultimate advantages thus secured for the future. Under capitalism the proprietor disposes of the surplus-value while in centralist socialism the surplus-value is absorbed into a remote, anonymous fund administered by the State. When personal income is directly and tangibly dependent on the income of the undertaking, and when this income is directly linked with the undertaking's productive potential and the modernity of its equipment, then investment becomes no less important to the worker than his immediate wage. This is not by any means a theoretical view since in Yugoslavia as a whole the number of failures attributable to insufficient investment and accumulation have been negligible.

The existence of problems, even of contradictions, cannot be disputed. Yet it is characteristic of the intellectual climate in Yugoslavia that the leaders themselves draw attention to these difficulties and shortcomings—in striking contrast to the habitual 'triumphalism' of centralized socialist régimes where criticism is normally regarded as an offence, if not incipient treason.

The resolution on socialist development at the Ninth

Congress of the League of Communists of Yugoslavia places the emphasis on this critical aspect: 'Social and economic reform, besides aggravating the contradictions inherent in society, has provoked an intense political and ideological ferment.'

Among the objective difficulties are the search for quick profits at the expense of long-term planning, exploitation of profit margins—with all its resulting distortions—on the part of enterprises favoured by circumstances, the drain of skilled manpower abroad, and unemployment induced by technology, as well as strikes where group interests are in opposition. There are, too, subjective difficulties such as a nostalgia for bureaucratic-technocratic relations, anarchistic praise of pure spontaneity at the expense of the conscious element, as well as antagonism between groups and interests.

If the socialist model of self-management is to bring about a complete liberation of labour from all alienation with no reversion to the domination either of private property or of centralized State control, the essential task is to establish a strong link between self-management and the forces of the new scientific and technological revolution.

This means passing through a new stage of self-management, namely *integration* which correlates the initiatives of the workers with scientific planning.

At the existing stage of socialist development in Yugoslavia integration corresponds to technological demands which, in any modern system, postulate the concentration of means. This in turn permits the formation of large economic units as bases indispensable to the advance of the scientific revolution.

Under capitalism, concentration operates in accordance with the laws of the jungle, the small being devoured and absorbed by the big.

In centralist socialism concentration is assumed from the outset; the whole of the nation's economy is regarded as one single enterprise centrally administered through a hierarchical organization, the units at the base being subordinated automatically to the authorities above.

The Yugoslav model tends towards a new type of integration. In place of unification of the mechanical type having a single centre whence all directives flow throughout the system, Yugoslavia is seeking to proceed from autonomous units to concentrations which will permit the establishment of larger, reciprocally self-adjusting groups —units, in short, that are cybernetic rather than mechanical.

This is a new and decisive stage. From the start, self-management, through the very fact of the historical circumstances of its birth and by way of reaction to the earlier centralist model, has been defined in negative terms as the opposite of centralism, as simple decentralization with its attendant dangers of a fragmented economy.

Some irresponsible theorists went so far as to invite ill-intentioned interpretations from abroad by speculating on Rousseauite individualism at a time when the leaders of the League of Yugoslav Communists were basing themselves more and more on an implicit philosophy according to which the subject of all rights is not the isolated, abstract individual of bourgeois humanism but rather the individual defined as producer by the whole of his relationship to the natural conditions which he transforms as also to the society which organizes his work and culture. The human essence, as Marx pointed out in his *Sixth Thesis on Feuerbach*, is not an abstraction inherent in the isolated individual. In its reality it is social relations as a whole.

Contrary to the many slanderous imputations levelled against Yugoslavia since 1948, her system of self-management has nothing to do with Proudhonian anarchism nor does it imply the economic and political disintegration of socialism.

While the system was in process of consolidation the

struggle to combat bureaucratic centralism and to promote the democratization of socialism was dialectically linked with an attempt at integration which made use of a number of channels—none of them, however, administrative.

First of all the Party. In a socialist model based on self-management the crucial problem is to overcome fundamental contradiction by the simultaneous realization of

a greater degree of free and autonomous activity for each worker,

a greater degree of conscious organization of social development,

the creative initiative of the masses and long-term scientific planning.

Hence the role of the Communist Party in such a system is more important than ever before; its essential task is to act as an integrating, synthesizing factor. The existence in a country of a large number of autonomous centres creates novel conditions unpropitious to illusions of 'economic harmony' such as those of Bastiat, the early nineteenth-century economist who thought that if everyone in a capitalist régime were to seek his own personal interest, the combined result would necessarily lead to an order in conformity with the interests of all.

The problems in a socialist system of self-management also have their root in autonomous subjects which are not individual proprietors but work units. The confrontation of the latter's interests does not produce, spontaneously and automatically, an order that is in conformity with the interests of society as a whole and its growth in the service of the full flowering of man. It may even happen that group interests give rise to clashes and contradictions as in the case of the coal-miners and the oil industry workers.

The task is to promote the general interest in these many autonomous centres and it is here that the Party's mission begins. Integration is possible only when the men and women in each autonomous centre of initiative and decision have acquired an awareness of the needs of overall social development. Moreover this awareness must be of an order that enables them to help the group as a whole, firstly to define the common social plan on the basis of the common criteria of human development and human progress, and secondly to ground itself on a common system of values permitting the conception of long-term objectives.

The Party, then, must act as an organized social consciousness capable of establishing the deep inner links which unite the historical demands of the workers at any given moment with the historical demands of scientific and technological development.

Only in this way can it perform its dual role: firstly to stimulate initiatives through continuous information and education, and secondly to effect the synthesis of these creative forces—to be, in other words, a factor that integrates, coordinates and guides.

The *avant-garde* role of the Party in a socialist model based on self-management implies a profound change in the concept of the Party and a radical break with what is termed its 'leading role' in a centralized, State-controlled model.

And this presupposes that the Party should first cease to identify itself with its own apparatus and then cease to identify the latter with the apparatus of the State.

As an organization of the proletarian class such a Party makes decisions but does not issue directives for their execution. Rather it is an ideological force which employs democratic methods and is itself democratically organized.

In other words it is coming less and less to be an organ of political power and increasingly an important ideological factor of social cohesion; for the members of the working class, whether manual or non-manual, it is their consciousness in its most lucid form.[12]

The Party cannot, *a priori*, lay claim to a monopoly of this consciousness nor can it legislate in the monopoly's name. It can only carry out its 'leading' role properly by providing continuous proof that it is the best means of stimulating, coordinating and orientating initiatives, and of ensuring that consciousness prevails over blind, uncontrolled spontaneity.

If it is to accomplish such a task the Party must work unremittingly to evolve its theoretical form and to assimilate the discoveries made by the natural sciences and the humanities. It must also engage in a continuous dialogue with history so as to be constantly aware of what is going on in the field of social reality; and in continuous dialogue, too, with differing expressions of opinion on the subject of social development.

It was thus that Marx defined the tasks of the 'League of Communists' and that is why, in 1952, the Yugoslav communists readopted the name for their organization.

This decision implied a profound change in the Party itself. It necessitated a struggle on two fronts, the first against those who wanted to keep the old bureaucratic, centralist system unchanged so that they could continue to rule by a series of directives, the second against those whose desire was to reduce the Party to a debating society for a would-be 'intellectual élite', without relation to the community's proper development.

These viewpoints, although in no way representing those of the League as a whole, were aired in the Press on a number of occasions thereby evoking facile and intemperate criticism from other Communist Parties which, since

12. In an article of the statutes of the League of Communists of Yugoslavia, the Party is defined as follows: 'The League of Communists is the revolutionary, ideological and political force, the organizer and the leader of the working class and the workers in the fight they are waging for socialism. The founding of a Communist classless society is the historical task and the final goal pursued by the League of Communists of Yugoslavia.'

they themselves forbade the publication of any opinions that were not those of the majority, at once interpreted the articles as being the official expression of the theses of the League of Yugoslav Communists. This 'reading', in the light of traditional dogmatisms, enabled the critics to maintain at one moment (when the article was of libertarian inspiration), that the Yugoslav communists were renouncing their *avant-garde* role, at another (when the article expressed nostalgia for Stalinism), that in Yugoslavia a 'healthy' opposition was upholding the 'principles of Leninism' in a country where there was nothing but strife and chaos.

There is no doubt that the Yugoslav communists have chosen a difficult road. It is simple enough when one has the power to give orders! But this is not the case in the new conception, as yet far from being realized in spite of the Yugoslav communists' unremitting efforts. In order to safeguard the rights of the class as a whole from usurpation by the Party, the authority of both Party and leaders is made wholly dependent on the arguments they put forward.

Faith in this Marxism and in this Leninism requires that the Party should keep a constant watch on itself lest there be any slackening of the intellectual tension needed to keep up with the dizzy rate of change in modern science, lest there be a failure to lend an attentive ear to the spontaneous aspirations of the masses. Moreover this faith requires an unfailing respect within the Party for the rights of the minority which in turn will permit the majority to choose between different available methods and variants of these methods when seeking the solution to particular problems. This is the only way in which the demands of scientific discussion and the demands of democratic discussion can be simultaneously met.

Unlike socialist models based on the centralist monopoly of Party and State, the self-administrative model, by the

very fact that it acknowledges the existence of contradictions and conflicts in its midst, allows, and indeed demands, that change and renewal should be effected by
means other than the spasmodic political explosions that
occur in statist, centralized models. In Yugoslavia nothing
is more striking than the opportunity given to all to express
freely their criticisms and suggestions. This liberty is not
without risks and disadvantages but for all the drawbacks
it does point to the strength of a system which is capable
of entertaining them. Again it points to the fundamental
adherence of the masses to that system since the latter is
able to subsist without recourse to official dogma or compulsion. Above all, this profound identity of democracy and
socialism allows for continuous self-criticism and ceaseless readaptation to new requirements.

According to one of Marx's texts which we have already
quoted, that is what distinguishes socialist democracy and
proletarian revolutions from the formal democracy born
of bourgeois revolutions: '. . . proletarian revolutions . . .
criticise themselves constantly, interrupt themselves continually in their own course, come back to the apparently
accomplished in order to begin it afresh, deride with unmerciful thoroughness the inadequacies, weaknesses and
paltrinesses of their first attempts, seem to throw down
their adversary only in order that he may draw new
strength from the earth and rise again, more gigantic,
before them, recoil ever and anon from the indefinite
prodigiousness of their own aims, until a situation has been
created which makes all turning back impossible . . .'[13]

Every social organization in the country having as its
aim the simultaneous development of self-management and
integration tends towards the same kind of working
methods as those used by the League of Communists of
Yugoslavia. For example there are the trade unions and the

13. Karl Marx, *The Eighteenth Brumaire of Louis Bonaparte,*
p. 100.

youth and cultural movements and also the Socialist Alliance which comprises all who wish to make an active contribution to the building of socialism.

At present the key problem in the development of self-management is that of integration, in other words the need for a concentration of means to allow for a large-scale exploitation of the opportunities presented by the new scientific and technological revolution. In a vital clause of the resolution carried at the Ninth Congress of the League of Communists of Yugoslavia under the title 'The Struggle for the Scientific and Cultural Revolution', the problem of possible contradictions was forcibly posed: 'Victory can only come to a system which is capable of ensuring the full development of the productive forces, of opening wide the door to the new dimensions of growth inherent in the modern scientific and technological revolution, to important technological systems, to automation, to cybernetics, to the rapid progress of science conceived as a direct productive force and to its application in technology . . . But if the rise of the new productive forces is not linked with liberation of labour, with democracy, with active participation in decision-making, if it fails to assume a human countenance and does not satisfy man's increasingly rich and complex needs, sooner or later it will become bogged down and will provoke violent social conflicts. The new productive potential will not be able to unleash to the full the powers that are latent within it; it will become a base for new forms of domination and for a technocratic monopoly. The expansion of the new productive forces and their place in the already evolved conditions of self-management—these today are the two aspects of progress in socialism. This is one of the new laws of the evolution of modern society.'[14]

This problem is not posed at all by the governing

14. Review, *Questions actuelles du socialisme*, No. 92, January-March 1969, p. 101.

bodies in the United States, nor is it adequately posed by the present Soviet leaders who refuse to recognize the contradiction.

By what means are the Yugoslav communists seeking to resolve it at the different levels—technological, political and theoretical?

So far as economics are concerned, we shall omit a detailed examination of the 'reform' decided on in 1965. Since our present intention is to give a broad outline of the socialist model of self-management, its functioning and orientation, it will be sufficient to recall the main import of the reform. This was intended to effect the transition from an extensive form of development to an intensive one and hence to prepare conditions in which every form of productive organization would correspond to rational standards appropriate to a developed country. The aim was to modernize the undertakings by encouraging integration and by permitting them to retain the major part (62 per cent) of the surplus-value as a guarantee of autonomy in their investment policy. The transformation of the banking system was to give the banks an increasingly active role in the general drive towards modernization and integration. The operation was a drastic one, for the hazardous process of integrating with the world market and entering into competition with the most highly-developed countries demanded an immediate monetary devaluation to the order of 66 per cent; on a basis of 1250 dinars to the dollar, instead of 750, a realistic equilibrium was re-established and convertibility became possible.

This abrupt entry into the world market involved a massive effort in the overhaul of production techniques and the raising of labour productivity and also a more stringently scientific policy of investment and a revision of the planning system.

At this economic level one of the most important factors in integration is the banking system.

In a centralized, statist model the role of the banks is reduced to a minimum, virtually to matters of cash and book-keeping since the bank merely carries out the decisions made by the central organs concerned with ministerial planning and the allocation of resources.

In the self-administrative model, where the State no longer plays this role, the banking system is much more complex. The bank becomes a highly important factor in integration since it stands at the focal point where the calls of the various undertakings in matters of credit and long-term investment coincide.

The bank, or rather the bank of banks—in other words the National Bank—cooperates with every organ in the life of the economy: the undertakings and work units, the planning commissions, the scientific research centres and the Federal Government (the governing body of the National Bank takes part in the meetings of the government and the commissions of the Federal Parliament).

In its operations the bank tries to adapt itself in every way to the conditions of self-management:

Its funds are derived primarily from the deposits of the undertakings and of private individuals but also from those of the State.

Control of the banks is ensured by councils composed of representatives both of the undertakings and the 'founder' work units who elect the director. The National Bank plays an important part in the realization of the plan, in the formulation of long-term economic policy, in the financing of cultural as of social programmes, in monetary policy and in external economic relations. At its head is a governor who is answerable to the Federal Assembly and to councils composed of experts, representatives of the work units and members of the bank's staff in varying proportions according to the functions of the council concerned. Schemes are in preparation to effect improvements in the present structure of the directing organs, so as to achieve a better correlation between the democratic demands of self-management and the scientific demands of planning.

Practical experience confirms the general law which follows from the great scientific and technological mutation, namely that there is no insurmountable contradiction between these two forms of demand. On the contrary, the more a country is developed, that is to say, the more its productive system is subjected to scientific development, the greater will be the pressure against administrative, authoritarian and centralized forms of decision-making. A scientific approach to the solution of problems postulates rather than excludes democratic modes of discussion.

With the bank as intermediary the State can thus steer production by means other than directives or administrative measures. It can for example encourage integration, today the crucial task, by creating economic conditions favourable for this purpose, by giving priority to undertakings in respect of federal investment or of guarantees enabling them to obtain foreign credits, and by tax concessions for work units whose integration leads to increased productivity.

In each case the bank is an intermediary rather than a distributor pure and simple. Under the direction of all the interested parties it makes a scientific study of requests for credit which it grants in accordance with the economy's general long-term policy and the profitability of the project. In short, it correlates plan and market so as to create the best possible conditions for expansion.

At the political level the basic unit for speeding up integration is the Commune. The name was chosen in order to emphasize those characteristics of the Paris Commune which it was intended to revive: assemblies that were at once active and deliberative, autonomous and administratively independent of a centralized, all-powerful State. Since 1953 the transfer to the Communes of the old powers of the Federal State and the Federated Republics has put real life into these local communities. In contrast to centralized systems where a central authority is responsible for education, the Communes enjoy full autonomy on this plane and are thus able to take the initiative in creating cadres adapted to the specific needs of the different regions. At this level, too, coordination and integration are not imposed by directives from 'above' but spring from the needs of the substructure.

The liberation of the economy from State control does not mean fragmentation; rather it is the creation of a unity more complex, more alive, and more free. Far from being abolished, the State now plays the role of intermediary, notably in cultural and economic matters, in order to help the work units and educational communities achieve a balance between immediately productive work and educational work. And this without erring either in the direction of the short-term practicalism of an undertaking on the one hand or the abstraction of an 'unworldly' college or university on the other—without sacrificing man's long-term cultural aspirations to the imperatives of profitability.

That is the form ultimately assumed by the problem considered at the theoretical level.

Self-management in Yugoslavia is now coming to the end of its decentralization phase and is approaching the next stage, namely that of integration. It is a trend which the Yugoslav communists intend to guide along the lines of self-management; not, that is to say, by directives from above but in accordance with objective economic laws and the needs actually experienced by the producers themselves.

In the matter of objective economic laws, integration is not invariably advantageous; the concentration of several craftsmen's workshops does not constitute a factory. The new units have to be born of economic necessity.

As to the producers, if they are to agree to the integration of their enterprise into a larger whole (the decision to integrate is invariably reached by way of a referendum among the workers concerned), there must be a change for the better, either at once or in the long term, in their working and living conditions.

In Yugoslavia it is within the framework of self-management that the theoretical and practical problems of planning and integration arise, problems whose solution will allow a full participation in the new scientific and technological revolution and make possible, within the context of human relations as a whole, the mutations which this revolution implies.

Both the plan-market dialectic and the worker's autonomy-scientific organization of production dialectic apply to every country and every régime.

Nowhere in the world is there an unadulterated 'market' based on the liberal principle of *laissez-faire*. We have shown the extent to which, even in the United States, the 'market' is encountering obstacles in the shape of intervention and internal regulations—obstacles that belie it.

Nowhere in the world is there total, strictly centralized planning. We have shown how the objective laws of the economy, notably the law of value (and this also in the Soviet Union), have asserted themselves even in the face of the most centralist and authoritarian pretensions of the State and how there has been a growing compulsion on economic reforms of recent years to make room for a market economy.

The task facing Yugoslavia, therefore, is by no means exceptional. These 'tensions' are to be found everywhere. It is merely a question of determining the 'model' in which they are least acute.

The Yugoslav system of self-management is an original

one: firstly because it is based upon work units consisting of large numbers of centres of decision capable of promoting economic initiatives; secondly because it refuses in principle to confuse planning with statist centralization and the acts of political intervention which are its consequence; lastly because it is concerned that there should be an organic link between planning on the one hand and the overall growth of the economy and of Yugoslav society on the other, and that this should result from a real increase in productivity rather than from external compulsion which, in a capitalist régime, may be exerted by private ownership or, in a centralized, socialist model, by the State.

The main feature of the Yugoslav system is that it does not proceed directly by way of central directives of a peremptory nature, but by indirect, economic and non-political methods. The tendency of these methods is to bring about the overall conditions in which each work unit can see clearly that its interest, both as a unit and in terms of its individual members, is to aim at a given type of production, to raise itself to a given level of integration. In a self-administrative system planning starts not with the fixing of norms but with price controls, the imposition of taxes, the terms governing import and export, etc., all of which affect the conduct of the producers.

It is hoped by this means to ensure that the plan will not be a rigid structure imposed upon the producers from without but rather that it will emanate from their needs as manifested in the market and, in the case of smaller units, from their planning initiatives. In this way the national plan would *comprise* those initiatives while endeavouring to coordinate individual and general interests, whether short or long term, by a process of self-regulation rather than by autocratic means.

The role of the State remains a very important one. But it is a guiding, synthesizing role. Initiatives and decisions do not all flow in one direction.

Furthermore the machinery, or rather the dialectic, of decision is a public matter.

By the dialectic of decision we mean that the elaboration of the plan is two-way: from top to bottom and from bottom to top.

There is no definite centre where economic planners prescribe what the undertakings are to produce and where they are to sell their goods.

The central organ in the plan is not a Ministry or a State authority but a scientific institution charged by the Federal Assembly with the construction of a model based on fully balanced, human, scientific and material resources which will permit maximum development. This institution is also required to plan the overall expansion of reproduction and to foresee modes of financing as also the general structure of production and consumption in the light of socialism's historical potential and perspective.

The 'model' is then put before the producers who thereafter are provided with the maximum *information* on the state of the internal and external market and on potential sales outlets, as also with *forecasts* of new requirements, in order that each undertaking shall have the opportunity of making the necessary preparations and adjustments or even of effecting a complete change-over. In this way the market can be protected from excessive upheavals.

The undertaking, however, decides autonomously on the basis of the forecasts received what its policy is to be regarding production schedules and planning as also its relations with other undertakings in such matters as joint schemes. These may involve the full or partial merging and integration of services, ranging from the promotion and coordination of sales to the organization of a more extensive and more automated production system and the introduction of joint research.

This does not mean that the State plays no further role, for it can intervene in ways that are economic rather than administrative by making use of instruments commonly used in a market economy to stimulate or check the activity of the hundreds of autonomous undertakings which confront one another in the market. By these same means it can also induce the undertakings to work towards the realization of the optimal model by approximating as closely as possible to the size that model lays down.

Direct financial intervention is, however, limited to what is strictly necessary since a system of joint investment carries the risk of a reversion to State ownership with its inherent dangers of centralization and bureaucracy. For reasons of principle and out of respect for the spirit of the self-administrative system, it is found preferable to encourage the formation of large economic associations supported by their own banks so that they may put into effect communal production and market development programmes. Thus, within the framework of planning freed from State control, the ground is being prepared for more thorough integration.

There are other ways in which the State can intervene, by price control, for example. But this is the exception rather than the rule—when, for instance, the question is one of maintaining the workers' standard of living (the measure affects foodstuffs and rents), or when an impediment to overall growth has to be eliminated (as in the case of the steel industry). Generally speaking price levels are established by the market in the traditional manner, the fundamental difference being that here the confrontation is between socialist undertakings rather than private interests. Regulation from above is only used as a last resort to restore equilibrium to the market, not to suppress it.

Action is also possible by way of export subsidies and taxes on imports and by State guarantees for the procurement of foreign capital, the production units themselves being given complete freedom to conduct their own negotiations with foreign firms and even to set up joint companies.

In the latter instance the only conditions are that 51 per cent of the capital must be Yugoslav and that under no circumstances must foreign participation obtrude upon the socialist relations of production within the enterprise.

Finally, taxation is a means of adjusting and balancing the portion of the surplus-value devoted to consumption and the portion devoted to investment.

At the present time the only legally binding limitations on the movement of merchandise, manpower and capital are those imposed on the expansion of private ownership of the means of production so as to obviate a return to the exploitation of the labour of others. Where private property is concerned the law forbids the ownership of more than four acres of land and the employment of more than five wage-earners in an hotel or in an industrial, commercial or transport undertaking. One of the problems now being examined is to determine whether it would not be more effective, in this field also, to apply economic methods rather than legal restrictions, and to use fiscal measures to limit opportunities for capitalization.

To sum up, planning in Yugoslavia is not a function of the State but the essential right enjoyed by every citizen within the framework of self-management.

When planning has finally been divorced from the State it assumes a more genuinely socialist character. It becomes less and less hierarchical and increasingly self-regulating through a system of interdependence consciously and freely agreed on by the work units. That is why it is untrue to say that self-management hinders the progress of technological innovation although the latter demands large-scale investment and long-term planning. On the contrary the real obstacle to the full expansion of the self-administrative model now is the low level of technology.

This is a most important point to remember when countering the prejudiced view that self-management is a consequence of under-development, and little more than a palliative. Indeed self-management is the only way in which a highly developed society can organize human relations in general and the relations of production in particular.

At the present stage one of the main preoccupations of the League of Yugoslav Communists is to move in the direction of a more advanced form of integration, the form, that is, best suited to the demands of the new scientific and technological revolution. This means the integration of science with social practice generally, and the integration of scientific research and teaching at all levels with social creativity as a whole. And this not simply as a way of achieving the optimal expansion of the economy but as a means of developing all social activities with a view to the attainment of a socialist society in which the demands of science and the demands of democracy are harmoniously compounded.

State intervention in this field is not excluded *a priori*; the laws and regulations, however, are regarded as part of a more general action based on objective necessity rather than on subjective choice.

The mutations proceeding from the new scientific and technological revolution are therefore primarily dependent on the initiatives of the work units, whether these are large, self-managed, integration-orientated undertakings or non-economic organizations such as scientific research centres and educational communities.

For the measures taken by the State are not properly effective unless they are elicited by some definite development of the productive forces and of productivity. They must come about organically.

Without any doubt increasingly rapid integration is the fundamental requirement for scientific and technological progress. But the rate of this integration cannot be 'forced' by State directives or by political and ideological pressure without regard for economic laws. For integration does not necessarily imply progress, even when accompanied by the modernization of equipment. If, for example, the new technology cannot be put to rational use because of too small a market at home or an absence of outlets abroad, the investment made will remain idle and unprofitable.

There must be an interdependence between all the factors of growth before coordination and synthesis can begin: integration must be an organic product of economic development.

The decisive factor in this field is not the concentration of capital by way of simple accretion but greater labour productivity in accordance with internal needs and with the country's assimilation into the international division of labour.

The fact that over the last fifteen years Yugoslavia has ranked among the group of countries having the fastest rate of development, in spite of her heavy initial handicap, is the best indication that self-management, far from being a hindrance to technological progress, in fact creates the most favourable conditions for it.

The principle of self-management is realized at the basic level of the 'workers' councils', thence becoming a general principle for the organization of society, a principle which gradually transforms the whole of human relations, starting at the political level.

In Yugoslavia criticism of Stalinism and the centralist, State-controlled model ranges from the economic and social base to the political superstructure. Its point of departure is quite clearly the distinction (not the earlier confusion) between social ownership and State ownership.

The concept of State ownership is highly contradictory: State ownership connotes at once the abolition of capitalist private ownership of the means of production, and the abolition of the exploitation of wage labour on which this mode of ownership is based. But it is also a form of ownership which perpetuates the alienation of the means of production with respect to the worker by excluding him not only from decisions affecting production and the allocation of surplus-value but also from the general administration of the economy.

Marx touched on the root of political alienation when he pointed to the opposition in a capitalist régime between private interests and public interests leading to confusion over man's double role.

Political liberation, in other words emancipation in respect of a State where the worker plays only a fictitious role, has been defined by Marx as follows: 'Human emancipation will be complete only when man . . . has recognized and organized his own powers as social powers so that he no longer separates this social power from himself as political power.'[15]

State ownership does not permit the 'socialization' of political activities nor does it provide for decisions to be made at worker level. It never gets beyond the limits of indirect democracy in which all decision-making is the monopoly of a body of deputies who act as intermediaries between the worker and the decision. The worker, although formally a voter, is thus relegated to a passive role in matters of political decision-making.

The crucial problem in a socialist democracy is to bring decision-making, both political and economic, closer to the worker who might otherwise be subordinated to extraneous political forces personified by a remote, anonymous State.

Thus self-management by the workers' councils is incompatible with a centralized all-powerful State whose administrative machinery runs counter to objective economic laws and the autonomy of the workers.

During the transitional period of socialist construction alienation cannot be overcome either by surrender to the blind anarchistic forces that confront each other in every market economy, or by reversion to the administrative

15. Karl Marx, 'The Jewish Question' in *Early Writings*, p. 31.

methods of a State machine which is above, and external to, the workers.

The aim of conscious political action is to ensure that the long-term requirements of the development of socialist, social relations remain paramount.

The primary objectives of political power, when once this is wielded by the working class, are as follows: to protect the social form of ownership from all attempts by individuals or groups to subject it to private control or to debase it in any way; to prevent any form of appropriation other than that based on labour; so to equalize the conditions of economic activity that those economic units which at the outset enjoy special advantages, either of location or equipment, do not take advantage of their situation at the expense of the others.

In what ways, then, is it possible to attain these objectives which are fundamental to a socialist democracy?

In accordance with the 1963 Constitution, decision-making is brought closer to the worker first by setting up self-managed work communities both inside and outside the sphere of material production. As we have already seen, those outside include the educational communities, the universities and the health and social security services, all of which are self-managed. Hence decisions can be made, without the restraint of State intervention, by those who have a direct interest in the problems and are better able to solve them than some remote body of bureaucrats.

In the same way, when the work unit is too extensive to be managed directly by all its members, the delegation of authority to their representatives is effected not horizontally on a territorial basis but vertically by functional integration; the problems of each branch of activity are settled not by a non-specialist parliamentarian for whom political decision-making has become a profession, but by a member of the community of interests who in all probability will continue to follow his career. Unlike a professional politician he is personally involved in the problems of those who have elected him and who pursue the same activities as himself.

We have already laid stress on another democratic measure which is necessary if decisions are to be made as close as possible to the substructure. This is decentralization, in other words, a broad measure of autonomy for the Communes and the transfer to them of nearly everything which, in a capitalist country or a centralized, socialist model, would come within the province of the State. Restrictions on the Communes by the State machine have been further relaxed to the extent that functions which would elsewhere be carried out by the agencies or Ministries of the State here devolve on the work communities or those having common interests.

This system of direct democracy is not altogether unlike the model of the Paris Commune in which Marx descried an essential feature of socialist democracy—a feature adopted by Lenin for the 'Soviets'—namely the assembly which does not simply deliberate but also acts, thus eliminating the dualism between legislature and executive.

Another original feature of the Yugoslav political system is the attempt to ensure direct socialist democracy by preventing one single political party or a plurality of parties from intervening as intermediaries between members of society and decision-making.

Elsewhere the various systems of representation evolved up till now have comprised either several rival parliamentary parties or a single party that has become the nucleus of the State. In each case these parties enjoy a monopoly of political decision. According to the Yugoslav conception, democracy cannot be achieved either by a plurality of parties disputing the power of the State or by the confusion of the State with one single party.

The political and ideological force constituted by the

League of Yugoslav Communists strives to remain an integral part of the self-administrative system in which direct democracy is being achieved by numerous centres of initiative and decision. In the first place a person who holds a leading position in the State may not hold a similar position in the Party.[16] Next, the Party is not entrusted with the administration of affairs; once absolved from this duty, which would lead it in the direction of practicalism, its identification with the State apparatus becomes progressively less. Nor does the Party make prior decisions which the assemblies or the government do no more than ratify.

Changes in the relations between State and Party are bound up with changes in the role of the State itself. In administrative socialism engendered by the monopoly of State ownership all work communities are subject to the bureaucratic control of the State apparatus and the Party. When property is socialized its basic attributes (disposal of surplus-value, organization of work, etc.) are transferred to the work communities, not to the State; decisions, including those made in the representative assemblies whose deputies are elected on essentially professional grounds by the workers in the corresponding branches of activity, are not made by one or several parties acting as intermediaries but are made directly by those who are immediately concerned. The actual choice of deputies is not determined by any party.

In the field of national representation there are five assemblies or chambers which, far from having comprehensive powers, make their decisions in close consultation with the communities whence they have sprung. Three of these chambers correspond to the three main labour arteries: the Economic Chamber, the Chamber of Education and Culture and the Chamber of Welfare and Health. Next there is the Organizational-Political Chamber elected by the

16. Tito is the one provisional exception.

Communes, and finally, since the Yugoslav Federation comprises many peoples, a Chamber of Nationalities consisting of an equal number of deputies from each of the Republican Assemblies.[17]

These are the methods adopted to ensure as much autonomy as possible in the making of decisions.

And these methods imply a great deal of faith in man.

They also appear to have made possible the large-scale politicization of the masses. In company with the League of Communists, the Socialist Alliance—a supra-ideological group with eight to ten million members—plays an extremely important role in the task of attaining socialism's long-term objectives. This it does, not by acting as a relay between the masses and the State, but as the institutional expression of the political activity of those masses, as the instrument which synthesizes the initiatives of the substructure, and lastly as the conscious organization of the political effort to define common goals and values and reconcile the differences of any groups whose interests do not converge spontaneously.

These notes do not purport to be a study of the Yugoslav system or of the way it works. Rather, we have tried to give a broad outline of the 'model', without any attempt to idealize what is actually taking place in the country or to provide an apologia for it. Nor have we in any way identified actual practice with the proposed norm.

A valid assessment of the specifically Yugoslav realization of the model would require a stringent comparative study of results and performance in all spheres of social

17. Our sole purpose here in examining the concrete functioning of the Yugoslav self-administrative model is to discover which of its features have universal validity. Hence we have deliberately eschewed problems that are specifically Yugoslav, notably the multi-national question and its democratic solution by the federal régime, as also the problem of the under-developed areas which the country will have to settle within her own frontiers— her 'Third World problem'.

activity both in capitalist countries and in other socialist countries.

That was not our purpose here. All we were concerned with was to isolate those features peculiar to a socialist model based on self-management, firstly in order to achieve the necessary critical detachment towards the statist model long regarded as the only admissible and only possible one; secondly to distinguish the former from the historical conditions of its realization so as to be able to examine its general validity and the possibilities it might offer under other conditions.

In the course of our reflections it has become apparent that the realization of this model in Yugoslavia was hampered primarily by the initial state of under-development. It would be rash indeed to assess the value of a model on the basis of one isolated experiment in a country which started off with a national income equivalent to 150 dollars per head of population, an income that today is still no more than 500 or 600 dollars.

There are also other circumstances which should be taken into consideration: the fact that initially the turn to self-management was a reaction against statist central-ism so that for long the emphasis lay on the more polemical and negative aspects and on a kind of 'phobia' of central-ization, on a systematic mistrust of the State. Thus the main feature of self-management appeared to be decentral-ization although it was in fact essentially democratization, the participation of all the workers in decision-making, while the model of socialism it inspired was a dialectical relationship between autonomy and integration. This has become clearly apparent over the last three years, high-lighted as they have been by the Economic Reform of 1966 and the Ninth Congress of the League of Yugoslav Communists in 1969.

This being said, we can go on to pose the essential problem of the universal validity of the 'model' so ably conceived and realized by the Yugoslavs under the most unfavourable historical conditions.

What possibilities might not this model hold out in a country with a developed economy and technology, a high cultural standard, a skilled, educated working class, and democratic bourgeois traditions?

Might it not provide the most favourable conditions for socialist penetration and for the acceptance of the mutations stemming from the new scientific and technological revolution?

# 5 The Socialist Future of France—
Prospects and Initiatives

In defining France's own initiatives, we shall not revert to the fundamental criticism of monopoly capitalism nor to the specific imprints it has left on Gaullist policy. This we have already analysed in detail in *Pour un modèle français du socialisme*,[1] and we have nothing further either to add or delete.

The Gaullist régime has, in its fashion, attempted to find an answer to the problems posed by the new scientific and technological revolution. Having assessed the importance of technologists as a class, it was at pains to win them over and to weld them into one bloc with the masters of the monopolies and the technocrats. This endeavour to create an 'historic bloc' ran counter to historical necessity since the technological strata cannot play their full role in an economy whose sole motive is profit. We have already pointed out[2] the fundamental contradiction arising from what we have termed the 'dual rationale': on the one hand, the capitalist rationale, the logical basis essential to the maximization of profits; on the other, the technological rationale, the logical basis essential to the achievement of the optimal growth of the economic apparatus. This latter rationale can only evolve unimpeded in a system which links the requirements of a full development of the new scientific and technological revolution with the require-

1. Roger Garaudy, *Pour un modèle français du socialisme*, Part III, 'Réflexions sur les formes actuelles du capitalisme', pp. 205-300.
2. Ibid.

ment that this same development should be put to use, not to increase the profits of the few but to satisfy the needs of all.

At bottom the fall of General de Gaulle is an expression of the failure of this endeavour. The crisis of May and June, with its mass demonstrations by students and technological cadres, showed, indeed, to what extent the endeavour ran counter to history.

Since then neither government nor employers have done anything to show that they have understood the lesson of that moment of French history.

The reversion to outmoded practices was prompted by a shabby concern to snatch back from the students, the cadres, the working class and even the middle classes such concessions as had been made under pressure in May. And just as the devaluation of 1937 was the bosses' revenge for the 1936 labour strikes, so the devaluation of 1969 was their revenge for the strikes and demonstrations of May 1968.

Now the events of May and June 1968, by increasing purchasing power and widening the home market, had boosted the economy to an extent that surprised even the employers; in September 1969 the National Institute of Statistics had certified that France's industrial costs were no higher than those of her other European partners, and both the report of the nation's Accounts Commission and the O.E.C.D. *Bulletin* had established that the rise in wages was being offset by increased productivity. In spite of all this, French capitalism (and its mouthpiece, the French government) persisted in looking to the past. It was a shabby policy based upon reprisal in the form of devaluation, upon speculation commensurate with a moneylending capital, involving up to four thousand million dollars and assured of immunity by the government, and finally upon an ideology, as outmoded as the policy itself, intended to mask the fundamental fact : the slowing down of the French productive apparatus in consequence of an unavowed Malthusianism. Hence the Finance Minister's surprising declaration that the French consumed too much, leaving no margin for export, and the Prime Minister's proclamation of a 'new society', based on a paltry bonus in the form of 'compulsory savings' and a few shares for the workers.

To speak of a 'new society' in these terms was a fine bit of lip service paid by vice to virtue. Indeed nothing was more necessary than a 'new society'. But how could it be new if there was no intention of touching either the authority or the profits of the employers?

No way will be found out of the blind alley nor can there be any prospect of a 'new society' so long as the manual and non-manual workers take no part:

in decision-making,

in the distribution of surplus-value;

so long, that is, as capitalism and its underlying principles remain uncontested.

That is why, in this chapter on France's own initiatives, we shall consider not the present government which is ruled out by reason of its regressive policy, but the Opposition and within this Opposition the only force that can inspire it—the French Communist Party. This Party alone, carrying the weight that it does in the working class, is powerful enough to adopt the initiatives which will enable the Opposition and the country itself to emerge from the impasse.

But the Party must still set itself the essential task of breaking free from its ghetto. And without doubt there are powerful external forces which are at pains to keep it there. The fact remains, however, that since the Liberation a quarter of a century ago, the Party, although contriving to maintain its position despite all the hatred and slander, despite all the tricks and violence perpetrated by the enemies of the working class, has yet to go over to the offensive, to carry along with it the Opposition as a whole and, in concert with that Opposition, to form an active force responsible for the nation's destiny.

It would be altogether unjust to imagine that the Party is solely, or even principally, to blame for this situation, for which there are, indeed, objective reasons, namely the relative strength of the classes that confront each other and also the intrigues of those within the working class itself who become the auxiliaries of capital and the upholders of its ideology.

Incontestable though all of this may be, it does not by any means exclude an examination of the possible ways in which the Party can react more effectively to this pressure, can break out of the circle and so reach its goal.

The problem is a complex one.


The political situation in France is made up of paradoxes.

In the introduction to this book we recalled those on which our reflections are based:

an Opposition that is powerless yet in the majority,

within this Opposition a Communist Party that is powerless yet in the majority,

a Communist Party whose cooperation is essential for constructive action while this in turn postulates a profound transformation of that Party.

The Party's way out of the impasse is not a change of programme, still less a change of objective, but rather a transformation of its method and style of operating so that, instead of remaining simply a compact force feared and shunned by its enemies, it will become the living, dynamic centre of French life as it moves forward into the future.

What, then, if this goal is to be achieved or at least approached, are the main initiatives which could open up new prospects for the Communist Party, for the Opposition and, finally, for France herself?

1. *The first initiative should be to base strategy and tactics*

*on a scientific analysis of present-day class relations in France.*

If we are to confront the problem in all its immediacy, we cannot go on repeating parrot-fashion, as if these were still the days of the Paris Commune or the 1917 Revolution, that a socialist revolution can only be victorious if a revolt by the workers is accompanied by a peasant uprising. Nor can we continue to speak of the working class as if it was composed exclusively of manual workers.

The role of scientific socialism is to demonstrate that the advent of socialism is an historical necessity and, on the basis of a rigorous study of the contradictions existing at each moment of history, to determine what can be done.

This was the example set by Marx in *Capital*.

When Lenin sought to define Russia's path towards socialism he founded his argument on an analysis of 'The Development of Capitalism in Russia'.

The basis of a study which poses the problem of the transition to socialism must needs be a fundamental analysis of the relative strength of the classes in France today, an analysis not only of the intensification of capitalism's old contradictions (already described by Marx) but also of *new contradictions* in the capitalist system. These contradictions did not exist either in the lifetime of Marx or in Lenin's day, but first made their appearance in the middle of the twentieth century with the second industrial revolution, a revolution dominated by the application of cybernetics to production and to economic administration.

The first task is to take the measure of this *tremendous mutation* with a view to defining perspectives and adapting strategy and tactics to a situation that is profoundly new.

What changes have come about in class relations over the last twenty years?

First, the working class.

Up to the middle of the twentieth century and in France

up to about 1955-56, the general tendency was towards a fall-off in the growth of skilled workers, i.e. the proportion of unskilled workers was increasing.

During the last fifteen years this trend has been in process of reversal.

Taking 100 as a basis:

the number of unskilled workers has risen in fifteen years from 100 to 108,

whereas the number of skilled workers has risen from 100 to 131,

the number of engineers from 100 to 148,

of higher cadres from 100 to 151,

of technologists from 100 to 171.

In the chapter dealing with the new scientific and technological revolution we considered the consequences arising therefrom:

a profound change in the very notion of professional skills and the increasing share of culture generally in these skills;

the growing importance of brainwork in what Marx called the 'collective labourer'.

The mutation now taking place implies not only an increase in the number of research workers, engineers, cadres and technologists but also a rapid expansion of many of the 'intellectual' strata, notably in teaching and in the administrative cadres of public and private enterprises.

From the censuses of 1954 and 1962 we learn that the number of wage-earning non-manual workers increased, in round figures, from 3 million to over 4 million during those eight years, while the peasant population decreased from 4 million to 3 million over the same period.

From the class aspect what do these social strata now in process of expansion represent?

When Marx defined the concept of the 'collective labourer' in the final volume of *Capital* (*Theories of Sur-*

*plus-Value*), he gave a brief analysis of the relation of the working class to the engineers and technologists: 'Taken as a whole these labourers (unskilled workers, labourers, *engineers* who work primarily with their brains, and others), in as much as they are collective producers, constitute a living machine. If we consider production in its entirety, they exchange their labour for capital and reproduce the capitalist's money in the form of capital . . . The position of each of these men, particularly with regard to capital, remains that of a wage labourer, of a productive labourer in the specific sense of the word.'[3]

In the second volume of *Capital*[4] he had already pointed out that 'As in the natural body head and hand wait upon each other, so the labour-process unites the labour of the hand with that of the head . . . The product ceases to be the direct product of the individual, and becomes a social product, produced in common by a *collective labourer* [my italics], i.e. by a combination of workmen, each of whom takes only a part, greater or less, in the manipulation of the subject of their labour. As the cooperative character of the labour-process becomes more and more marked, so, as a necessary consequence, does our notion of productive labour, and of its agent, the productive labourer, become extended.'

The evolution of history precludes us from including non-manual workers as a body among the middle classes, the more so since the steady decline of certain sections (peasants, artisans, small shopkeepers) goes hand in hand with the advance of capitalism, while the growth of the non-manual strata continually gathers momentum.

This progress will be even more marked in a socialist régime where, in direct contrast to the middle classes, these

3. Karl Marx, *Histoire des doctrines économiques*, ed. Costes, Vol. II, p. 213 (Appendix, 'The idea of productive labour').

4. Karl Marx, *Capital*, Vol. 2, Ch. XVI, 'Absolute and Relative Surplus-Value'.

strata will become increasingly important both numerically and strategically.

Does that mean that, if we exclude them *en bloc* from the middle classes, we ought to place them *en bloc* in the working class?

From a theoretical point of view that would be a less serious error but it would not constitute a precise scientific definition. Not simply because their standard of living is more akin to that of the bourgeoisie or because their ideology bears the latter's imprint—this being irrelevant to fundamental Marxist criteria of class distinction—but above all because it will often be difficult, even allowing for the new conditions affecting the production of surplus-value, to draw the line between those who take part in the production of surplus-value and those who benefit from its distribution. Do teachers, for example, produce surplus-value? Do students? Generally speaking the problem is posed in a way that is too mechanistic, too narrow, and with insufficient awareness of the new conditions affecting production in the era of the new scientific and technological revolution.

It is sometimes said that teaching is the simple reproduction of labour-power. That was true of traditional apprenticeships where a worker was trained to carry out the same specialized tasks as his predecessors. And much the same applies to the Napoleonic *lycées* whose original purpose was to provide cadres for the economy and the State, to instil, by a process of simple reproduction, the aptitudes necessary to carry out a predetermined task. In the same way the primary school imparted the knowledge needed by production's 'rank and file'.

Today this attitude no longer holds good. In an era when one of the most evident consequences of the great mutation has been a twofold increase in knowledge within the space of ten years, when it is becoming less and less possible to rest content with a once-for-all period of training or apprenticeship, when the refresher courses needed for constant readaptation to scientific and technological innovations take place at ever more frequent intervals, then teaching ceases to be simple reproduction and instead becomes *expanded reproduction*. As such it comes to be increasingly a producer of surplus-value.

At the same time, the problem must be rethought from the point of view not only of the teachers but also of those who are taught. It might be said of a worker, technologist or engineer who goes on a refresher course that he ceases to be a producer of surplus-value for the period he is away from his job. Yet this would be a very short-sighted view and one, furthermore, contrary to the analyses made by Marx who went beyond the categories of a mechanistic, linear causality when studying the production of surplus-value. Rather, it is a case of tackling the fundamental problem, posed by Marx, of the 'collective labourer', of making a structural analysis of this 'collective labourer' in an era when science is becoming more and more a directly productive force. At the present stage not only refresher courses but also permanent education, as well as teaching as such, are important factors in expanded reproduction and in the creation of surplus-value.

Yet this is not the essential problem.

What is essential is to draw a clear, scientifically based distinction between the social strata. There are those with which the working class can form an alliance although *in principle* their class interests may be different. Such is the case with the lower middle classes of the classical type (small landed peasants, artisans, small shopkeepers). They are the owners of their means of production, they produce no surplus-value and, as a rule, they are ideologically backward-looking. But by virtue of the fact that they are gradually being ousted by large capital and by the monopolies, they have objective reasons for allying themselves with the working class against those monopolies.

With the bulk of the non-manual workers the problem is posed otherwise. In spite of the wide range of strata comprised within this category in the historical conditions of State-monopolistic capitalism, most of them—indeed the most characteristic part—are sellers of their intellectual labour-power and, as presaged by Marx, either direct or indirect producers of surplus-value. Included here are the engineers, technologists, research workers, and even a large proportion of the managerial cadres in the public and private sectors. They do not own their means of production and whatever their standard of living or their outlook—this last deriving from their social origins—their objective interests do not differ *in principle* from those of the working class. There are, on the contrary, some objective elements that converge.

These social strata cannot however simply be identified with the working class, nor can the problem of an alliance in their case be expressed in the same terms as in the case of the lower middle classes.

With the traditional lower middle classes tactical[5] alliances can be formed. With broad sections of the non-manual workers the alliance will rather be a strategic one, if not actually a progressive fusion that leads to the construction and full development of socialism.

It was to emphasize this twofold difference that in my book *Pour un modèle français du socialisme* I took up and gave a new content to the concept of the 'historic bloc' outlined by Gramsci.

The working class and these non-manual workers cannot have the same relations with respect to an alliance as had the working class and the lower middle classes in the past,

5. 'Tactical' does not here signify instability or deceit, since the victory of the working class opens up for these strata—particularly the peasants—the prospect of integration with socialism (by cooperative methods, for example), whereas all that a régime of monopolies has to offer them is eviction for the benefit of the more powerful.

nor do they constitute one and the same class. But they do constitute a new 'historic bloc' whose cohesion, ever more in evidence, will continue to gain strength in the future.

Attempts have been made to compare the 'historic bloc' as conceived by Gramsci with my own use of the term in this book. While I do not suggest that Gramsci and I are thinking along exactly the same lines, there is nevertheless a definite connection between his concept and mine. Gramsci's definition of the 'historic bloc' as unity between substructure and superstructure is contrasted with the definition ascribed to me, namely a coalition between social strata (in the event, between manual and non-manual workers).

In fact my intention was to get rid of the schema of a coalition between manual and non-manual workers conceived in accordance with the model of an alliance between workers and peasants.[6]

My starting point was the same as Gramsci's: 'An analysis of the organic links between the structure and the superstructures which, at a particular historical conjuncture, constitute a bloc that is differentiated and contradictory.' As opposed to any idea of 'coalition' or 'fusion' which would be purely circumstantial and subjective in an era when, as foreseen by Marx, science is becoming a leading force in production, it is an objective fact that a growing number of non-manual workers (notably engineers and research workers) are coming to form part of the 'collective labourer' and to evince class criteria corresponding to those applied by Marx when he defined the working class.

Having thus analysed, after Gramsci, the new development at substructure level of the historic reality of the working class (a class that cannot be confined to manual workers without indulging in an '*ouvriérisme*' very far removed from Marx's thought), an effort must be made at

6. See especially Roger Garaudy, *Pour un modèle français du socialisme*, p. 28.

superstructure level (particularly at the level of consciousness of these new relations) to bring our conception of the working class into harmony

with the logical consequences of that conception in regard to tactics, strategy and political organization,

with the new historical reality of the classes and their relations.

This is precisely what Gramsci proposes: 'An appropriate initiative is invariably necessary to free the economic impulse from the bonds of traditional policy, namely to change the political course of *certain forces which must be absorbed if a new historic bloc is to be realized* [my italics], a bloc that is economically and politically homogeneous and free from contradictions.'

Hence there is continuity rather than conflict between the term 'historic bloc' in the sense used by Gramsci and the sense used here. If the expression has a 'new content', it is because Gramsci is more often concerned with recalling the theoretical basis (the dialectical unity of substructure and superstructure) whereas we are inclined to place the emphasis on the consequences (a state of consciousness which permits the mustering of the forces necessary to bring about the political mutation demanded by this change in the substructure). The content is necessarily new since the crucial phenomenon in the France of 1969 (the new scientific and technological revolution which began about the middle of the century, bringing with it a new class status for certain categories of non-manual worker) was wholly absent from the Italy of the twenties.

This discussion would be pointless if it was nothing more than a learned debate about texts and terms; nor must we allow ourselves to lose sight of the fundamental realities, on the one hand the reality of the mutation and of the new concepts needed to grasp it, on the other, the reality of the revolutionary tasks which this mutation demands.

Indeed if we are to work out any form of strategy and tactics appropriate to present conditions in France we must of necessity base ourselves on a rigorous analysis of the 'historic bloc'.

Between the two constitutive elements of this 'historic bloc', in other words the working class as traditionally defined and the non-manual workers in all their diversity (some of the latter are now virtually integrated with the working class while others, the 'liberal professions' in particular, are still much closer to the middle classes) there exists a nexus. That nexus consists in a highly skilled section of workers who, by reason of changes that have come about in the actual definition of skill, find themselves in very close proximity to the technologists, the cadres and the engineers.

Even if these categories of worker are not yet numerically predominant, they do at the present stage constitute the strategic level decisive in cementing the new 'historic bloc'. It is an elementary principle of Marxist strategy that action should be based on something that is in process of emerging and developing.

Thus scientific and technological mutations have considerable social and economic implications and postulate profound political change.

2. The second necessary initiative follows from the first, namely a study of the new class relations which involves the rigorous definition of the new 'historic bloc' and which ultimately determines what claims are capable of forming its common denominator, thus ensuring a leading role within that bloc for the working class in its new expanded form.

In order to formulate these claims we would do well to consider the demonstrations of May and June 1968 which provide an exceptionally rich field of historical experience.

For the first time in our country's history, some eight or

nine million wage-earners brought the entire economic apparatus to a standstill. Qualitatively even more than quantitatively the phenomenon differed from the strikes of 1936 in that the demonstrations extended far beyond the working class, being particularly in evidence among the students.

In 1936 the president of the C.G.T., Benoît Frachon, emphasized that the strikes were the first major act of assertion in a period when capitalist concentration had been suddenly speeded up. Nowadays this process has become even more ruthless in response to the demands of increasing automation. In May 1968 France experienced her first great strike of the cybernetic age.

This strike evinced two revealing characteristics:

Firstly, by reason of its extent, it was not simply a general strike involving only the working class in the traditional sense of the term. It was the first rough prototype of a 'national strike' (the expression suggested by the General Secretary of the Spanish Communist Party, Santiago Carillo) in which the new elements of the working class (in its broader, modern sense) took part, as also many cadres of engineers, students, officials and other sections of society. Moreover this strike was not directed solely against the exploitation of labour but also against its *alienation*. These are new elements having considerable theoretical and practical importance in an analysis of what became apparent in May and June 1968. One shrewd observer, M. Henri Callat, wrote:

'In May 1968 it was not simply the worker *qua* immediate labour-power who had revolted; rather it was the collective labourer" *qua* "appropriation of its productive force as a whole" which, perhaps for the first time in an industrially developed country, had manifested itself with such vigour.'

Without doubt the miners' strikes of 1963 and subsequently the Neyrpic strike in Grenoble had been manifestations of this new phenomenon but never to the nation-wide extent of the demonstrations of May and June 1968. These underlined the basic fact that the actual development of technology today tends to create a close link between wage claims and the indictment of the very principle of the capitalist system, a system which bars the workers from the management of their labour.

As we have already stressed, the novel fact to emerge since 1936 is that although, twenty years ago and more, the requirements of technological and economic development were running counter to the requirements of democracy, at the present stage both are proceeding in the same direction.

In its issue of September-October 1968, *Option*, the journal of the General Union of Engineers and Cadres in the C.G.T. which has been at pains to show how the concerns of the cadres integrate with the whole movement of the exploited, made the noteworthy point that it would be unrealistic and false to oppose the claims of the non-cadre workers to those of the cadres on the assumption that millions of the former went on strike merely to obtain higher wages for themselves, whereas the cadres confined themselves to demands for a share in the formulation of plans and policies directly related to, or comprising, their own sectors.

In reality there was in either case a dialectical interplay between the claims represented by these two poles even if, in particular instances, the emphasis was differently placed.

It is significant that in the most advanced sectors such as electronics, petrochemicals and the aerospace industries, the two elements were closely linked:

The non-cadre workers in Pétroles d'Aquitaine demanded an organization 'that would define their own responsibility in society as a whole'.

On 20 May the main platform of the cadres at the Suresnes factory of Sud-Aviation was 'effective and democratic participation in the management of the enterprise', but by the end of June the emphasis had shifted to the question of wages.

On 28 May and 30 May respectively the cadres in Saviem and in Kléber-Colombes focused their claims on the right to information and to participation in the management.

At Thomson-Houston, Hotchkiss and Brandt, both workers and cadres, having abstracted from the strike movement of May 1968 what they described as its 'profound if not historic originality', laid stress on the claims of initiative, responsibility and dignity against the 'monarchical society' as constituted by the enterprises.

We could quote many more examples from May and June 1968 of this tendency on the part of the cadres, as also on that of broad sections within the working class, to make participation (even though the sense of the word has been corrupted by authority) the main theme and motive force of their claims.

The term participation does, of course, cover a number of very diverse realities ranging from a straightforward extension of trade union rights to workers' control in the sphere of economic orientation and administration, the latter being a state of affairs that can only come about in a socialist régime.

Above all we must not confuse 'participation' and 'self-management' between which there is a fundamental difference: self-management can only begin after the abolition of private ownership of the major means of production. The upper limits of 'participation' in the most favourable of cases—that is in a 'pre-revolutionary' situation—would be 'workers' control' as conceived and put into practice by Lenin during the transition from capitalism to socialism when management, though under the control of the workers, still remained in private hands.

This demand for participation, regarded by some as

synonymous with democracy within an enterprise, has been seized upon by governmental demagogues who have radically transformed its meaning and have rendered participation as 'class collaboration'.

It is significant, for example, that during the major strikes of May and June 1968 and at the Grenelle talks, the employers' main fear was to see the introduction of a 'parallel power'. Pressure from nine million striking workers was enough to enforce a guarantee of trade union rights within the enterprises. As for the government, it strove to canalize the powerful claims of democracy at enterprise level by itself taking up the slogan of participation, only to transmogrify it into a more generally acceptable version, namely the 'association of capital and labour'. Under this plan the workers were promised the right to information and consultation. But it was participation within very narrow limits. In a country where 'trade secrets' and hence the privilege of access to information were and still are the most effective means of inhibiting all interference with management, there seemed every probability that the right to information would be confined to the communication of non-confidential details rather than essential facts. Even more anodyne was 'consultation', whereby the workers or their delegates were entitled to give their opinion and put forward suggestions, but in a consultative capacity only; the question of recognizing the actual right of the workers to make decisions did not arise. Under these terms there was every likelihood that the proposed 'dialogue' would be used as a decoy, its purpose being simply to render more acceptable the decisions reached by this caricature of a consultative body and to lead, in the long run, to increased integration with existing authoritarian structures. Thus a wholly illusory form of participation would take over the role played by religion in the nineteenth century as an ideological instrument of integration.

There can be no doubt that participation served up in

this form was a decoy since the production relations of capitalism have remained inviolable and sacrosanct.

The first obstacle to any real change in a capitalist régime is private ownership of the means of production which confers on individual or collective proprietors the privilege of creating and controlling an enterprise, in the same way that in feudal times landed property conferred on its owners the privilege of leadership in war and the administration of justice.

Neither the trickery of the government nor that of the employers on the subject of 'participation' should cause us to lose sight of the class element which large numbers of workers, employees and cadres read into this word. It expresses their demand for a profound democratic transformation, for the transition from the formal democracy characteristic of all bourgeois régimes to a socialist democracy—a democracy, that is, which does not stop short at the factory gates where the employers' monarchical rule begins, but in fact extends to comprise the actual orientation and administration of the economy. To assert that in a capitalist régime such a claim is Utopian is to revert, but on a different plane, to the social-democratic argument about the 'vicious spiral of prices and wages' which was also founded on the view that in every capitalist régime all concessions are immediately and inexorably recouped by the employers. Yet it is, as Marx foresaw a century ago, the perpetual wage struggle that forges the strength of the working class. And today the same applies to the struggle over the claim for democracy within the enterprises, a struggle which to an increasing extent is becoming dialectically linked with the wage struggle.

It is well to lay stress on this link to avoid the pitfall presented by the illusion so tenaciously harboured by the leftists who have always believed that the 'struggle for jam on our bread is now a thing of the past' or that these wage claims are 'subordinate'. There is also the danger of falsely underestimating the aspirations to participation, confused though these may be. Even if the incumbents of the established order wish to make it the ideological badge of a policy of class collaboration, participation will still remain for many workers the expression of a demand for democracy at the economic level.

It is most important to be clearly aware of this new pattern in which alienation is becoming more and more a lived experience for the working class, for broad sections of the technologists and cadres, and for large numbers of non-manual workers generally. And this, not simply as a struggle against the exploitation of their labour-power, but also as a protest against the logic of a system whose aims, validity and meaning they are not permitted to discuss.

Only in this way is it possible to isolate the deep, intrinsic link between the aspirations of the students and the objectives of the working class even though the students' mode of expressing their demands is often unrealistic and anarchical, and even though their awareness of the link is often no more than an 'inverted reflection' of this historic movement. They experience the class contradictions of a capitalist régime as spiritual alienation at superstructure level, whereas the roots of the crisis lie in the system's economic contradictions, in the class relations of the substructure.

Here again *Option*, the journal of the engineers and cadres in the C.G.T., in its issue of November 1968, pages 39 and 40, shows very clearly why the cadres' protest is experienced as an extension of student protest: the students refuse to be integrated with an economic system which will form them into cadres in an enterprise whose sole criterion of good management is profit, while the cadres refuse to be cogs in a system which reduces the enterprise to a display of managerial techniques.

'The lot of the students—the future cadres—is closely

linked with that of the ex-student cadres. Both have to face the same problem, namely their assimilation into the productive apparatus: immediate assimilation for the technologists, engineers and cadres, potential assimilation for the students.'

The problem, that is, of their assimilation as cadres into a system where there is no opportunity to discuss goals.

By taking the measure of this profound historical mutation we shall also be able to establish on a correct basis the leading role to be enacted by the working class, in the exact and present definition of the term, under the conditions of the final decades of the twentieth century.

This in no way involves the abandonment or even the underestimation of quantitative claims in regard to wage-rates, the length of the working day, production levels and social security or, more generally, of all claims whose purpose is to oppose the exploitation of labour-power, since these remain intrinsically valid not only for the working class in the traditional sense (the manual workers) but also for the whole of the 'historic bloc'.

What is new and what made its demands so forcibly felt during May and June is the *qualitative* claim which questions the very essence of the capitalist régime—the struggle, that is, against the form of alienation which excludes the workers, whether manual or non-manual, from any share in decision-making within the enterprise. The claim for effective participation is, more than any other, the common denominator of all the claims put forward by the historic bloc as a whole, precisely because of its 'comprehensive' nature; it contains within itself all the other claims since their full realization is dependent on it. It also opens up another vista in the struggle for socialism by way of transition from participation to workers' control, and from workers' control to self-management.

But at this point the economic claim necessarily leads

on to the fundamental political problem, that of the State which sustains the existing production relations and also the form assumed by capitalist property.

In analysing that State a third initiative will be required in order to define the communists' attitude towards parties and Parliament.

3. State-monopoly capitalism has not fundamentally changed the nature of capitalism as such, for the major means of production and exchange still remain in the hands of the few, while labour is assuming an increasingly social character.

On both the economic and the political plane this development, far from refuting Marx's basic theories, verifies them anew for while earlier contradictions have not been resolved new contradictions have arisen.

The crucial factor that has emerged on the political plane is the increasing economic role played by the State, a role that can only serve to enhance the latter's repressive function.

During the past forty years and ever since the great crisis of 1929 which resulted in the kind of State intervention advocated by Keynes, the State's economic functions have grown significantly.

With the nationalization of the larger enterprises the State has entered the production cycle, and in the same way has become the country's principal banker by nationalizing or gaining control of the major financial institutions in both public and private sectors.

In a system that is progressing towards socialism nationalization, by competing with and ousting private enterprise, could be a useful means of exerting pressure on the private sector. This is far from being the case under the present régime, however, where nationalization is used by State capitalism to ensure the survival of the régime responsible for that nationalization, doing so the more effectively in as much as the proportion of public investment to overall investment in France is in the region of 40 per cent per annum.

Thus the chief function of the State is now quite other than it was in the nineteenth century, comprising as it does, firstly, the direction of capitalism's plans for expansion (elaborated in response to the challenge presented by the socialist economy); secondly, an operative and regulatory role in conjunction with State capitalism; and lastly, the responsibility, not only for technological development and the speed-up of the concentration of capital, but also for the negotiation of transactions at summit level between French capitalism and its counterparts in Europe and elsewhere. To this chief function of the State, indeed, all other functions—and notably repressive ones—must be accommodated.

Gaullism should undoubtedly be held responsible for hastening the maturation of State-monopoly capitalism in France in that it has accommodated the State to the demands made by the development of the big monopolies; Gaullism was thus an instrument of fate as well as of historical necessity.

The most prominent feature of that accommodation has been the erosion of parliamentary prerogatives.

In the age of liberal capitalism when State intervention in economic matters was purely negative, consisting in a 'watching brief' that helped capitalist development by removing legal obstacles, Parliament was a kind of tilting-ground for encounters between the different elements of the ruling classes—labour not being strongly represented at that time. The laws that were voted, in so far as they favoured and smoothed the way for one or the other of these elements, reflected the relative strength of the land-owning, industrial, commercial or banking interests.

With the emergence of imperialism Parliament was called upon to intervene in a rather more positive sense. Under pressure of more cohesive exterior forces and in spite of superficial differences within their own ranks, the ruling classes banded together against the two main factors which were henceforth to threaten them: at home, the rise of the working class whose influence in Parliament must be neutralized; abroad, competition from other imperialist powers which meant safeguarding the continuity of French imperialist policy against electoral vicissitudes. Yet Parliament still remained a council for the administration of the affairs of the bourgeoisie.

For a long time, indeed virtually until the eve of the Second World War and to some extent even up till 1958, these objectives could be met by traditional methods, namely corruption, electoral laws favourable to the ruling classes, ideological and political obfuscation through control of the organs of news and propaganda, and so forth.

Today the State's chief function, over and above its function of repression, is to organize the capitalist economy. Long-term planning is demanded by investments so vast as to be beyond the means of even private monopolies. In the cybernetic age forecasts have to be made and risks calculated fifteen or twenty years in advance.

The necessity for stability and continuity has definitively superseded those principles of free political competition which once constituted the charter of parliamentary democracy. Thus the political primacy of Parliament is doubly doomed:

for technological reasons,

for class reasons.

In the age of State-monopoly capitalism it is essential that major decisions should be taken by a State machine that is subject neither to traditional parliamentary vicissitudes, nor—and this is even more important—to debate and control by popular representation.

De Gaulle was in the main successful in fulfilling these twin requirements of the monopolies.

This implies profound consequences so far as the struggle for democracy and socialism is concerned.

First we should be absolutely clear that the subordinate role now being played by Parliament is no transient accident of history though this should not lead us to draw nihilist conclusions or revive the anarcho-syndicalism of another era.

As things are now in France, and with the new realignment of the classes, Parliament can still play an important part in the control of decisions through popular representation. Moreover the attainment of a majority in Parliament can be extremely useful for the purpose of rallying the masses and for supporting a democratic force on the threshold of socialism. But Parliament can no longer play an operative role in political life, whether in the attainment of power or in the administration of national affairs.

The reason why Parliament cannot play any real role in the conquest of power is because the vital core of the régime to be overthrown is no longer located there, so that the actual centres of decision and the monopolies' technocratic mechanisms of power cannot effectively be immobilized simply by grafting a new parliamentary majority on to a State machine whose nerve centres are elsewhere, and still less by means of gestures more reminiscent of the barricades of 1830 than of the present age.

This is not to suggest that no use should be made of elections and of Parliament on the one hand, or of mass demonstrations in the streets on the other. Rather we would emphasize that, since the State machine has become one vast economic apparatus, action to cripple it must first be taken in the economic field. Rallying the masses for electoral struggles, whether in Parliament or in the streets, still remains an effective means of reinforcing the struggle in the principal theatre of operations, namely the economy of a State whose chief function is economic.

The revolutionary struggle has to be carried into every field; not only into the field of politics but also into those of the economy and of culture. Marx and Lenin clearly recognized these three fields as distinct yet interdependent.

The specific historical conditions, however, in which socialist revolution has been effected—as, for instance, in China and Russia—have meant that the emphasis has always been placed on the chronological and hierarchical priority of the political struggle, often to the exclusion of anything else. This may have been necessary in countries that were, at the start, economically and technologically backward or where there was no bourgeois democratic tradition.

Such is not the case in highly developed countries where it is both possible and imperative to conduct the three forms of struggle simultaneously.

In Russia a working class formed by capitalism before the beginning of the new scientific and technological revolution and living in the repressive conditions of an autocratic régime was able, in a given conjuncture (war and defeat), first to seize political power and then, at least in Lenin's time, to give to the dictatorship of the proletariat the form of a socialist democracy. In the case of the French workers, both manual and non-manual, it would seem highly probable that this sequence might be reversed.

In the bourgeois revolution, as Lenin has indicated, the rising class already controlled the more advanced aspects of the economy at the time they seized political power. The socialist revolution in October reversed that order.

In the case of a socialist revolution in an advanced country, while it is probable that the factors would also be reversed, the nature of that reversal could clearly be different in that the workers would not obtain *ownership* of the principal means of production *before* obtaining political power. But what is entirely new in the France of 1969, as compared with the position in Russia in 1917, is the fact that the French workers, both manual and non-manual, all of whom are 'living' the fresh contradictions (which they will later 'think' and combat together), are *already*, in the course of the struggle for socialism, posing the problems that will be their own in the socialist society, more especially the problem of effective participation in the policy and administration of the State economy.

Like Marx, Lenin saw beyond the reality and the historical potential of his time and country when he posed the problem as follows: 'Take a practical apprenticeship in democracy . . . train the masses to participate effectively, directly and generally in the administration of the State; for this and *only this* will guarantee complete victory for the Revolution.'[7]

The objective conditions in which socialism was built after 1923 in the Soviet Union, as well as the mistakes made by Lenin's successors, fostered sometimes to the point of monstrosity the very perversion he had diagnosed in his lifetime, that of socialism constructed *for* the people instead of *by* the people.

As things are now in France, in the final decades of the twentieth century, the objective conditions for any such dichotomy between the 'seizure' of power and its democratic organization do not exist.

Again, and like Marx ahead of his time, Lenin envisaged that possibility, a possibility which has not proved capable of realization in his own country: 'The development of capitalism creates . . . the necessary *premises* for the true participation of all in the administration of the State. Among those premises are general education as already realized in several of the more advanced capitalist countries; next . . . the education and training of millions of men by the vast and complex socialized machinery of the

7. Lenin, *Works*, Vol. 24.

postal services, railways, large factories, the wholesale trade, banks, etc. Given such economic premises, it should be easy enough, once capitalists and officials have been overthrown, to replace them from one day to the next.'[8]

In our country today, where the new and unprecedented contradictions inherent in a developed form of capitalism are intensified by nervous tension and alienation rather than by immediate poverty (hunger, for example), the struggle against those contradictions already affords the workers certain opportunities for training themselves for socialism.

This means that socialist demands and the struggle for socialism now evince new features:

Criticism of the system, no matter to what field it is applied, goes hand in hand with discussions about possible alternatives to the system criticized.

The seizure of power does not take place only at the political level but simultaneously at all the levels (i.e. the economy, culture), at which the system is called in question by those who contest its very principle.

A socialist State born of a genuinely democratic demand for participation in all fields of social life can become a democratic State straight away, without first experiencing the kind of bureaucracy inevitable in a society where socialism has been achieved before the 'capitalist form' has reached its full term (thus compelling the new State to resort to extreme centralization of resources and powers, with all the tragedies that entails).

Hence we should undoubtedly seek to analyse, in the light of the conditions peculiar to France, the thesis put forward by the General Secretary of the Spanish Communist Party, Santiago Carillo, on the subject of a 'national strike'. This, let us hasten to add, has nothing in common with the hoary anarcho-syndicalist myth of the omnipotence of a 'general strike' since action of that kind today would only

8. Lenin, *Works*, Vol. 25.

serve to isolate one section of the workers and the masses generally.[9]

The May demonstrations by the working class, students and broad strata of cadres and officials—demonstrations which spread in June, though on rather a different scale, to the rural workers—did not constitute a 'national strike'. They were, however, the first indication of such an eventuality.

The revolutionary struggle cannot be restricted to an electoral and parliamentary struggle, nor can the latter even be regarded as essential to the former.

So much has Parliament's role been transformed and eroded that we must be careful not to identify peaceful methods of achieving the transition to socialism with parliamentary methods. Similarly, and for the same reason, we should be careful not to identify the problem of unity as such with the problem of the unity of the Left.

The term 'Left' has a generalized meaning synonymous with 'progressive force', but this should not lead us to forget that it first arose in a parliamentary context, and not just the actual physical context of the Assembly and its horseshoe arrangements of seats; there was a far deeper and more significant reason, the term being also linked with a particular concept of political parties—a concept which, today, is all but a dead letter.

To the Marxist a political party is the most organized and the most conscious fraction of a class or social stratum, voicing the interests of that class and organizing its struggle.

For many years, the various classes and social strata in France effectively depended for their political consciousness and structure on parties which possessed the means to

9. Cf. R. Garaudy, *Pour un modèle français du socialisme*, pp. 9, 210-311; also Santiago Carillo, *Problems of Socialism Today* (Lawrence & Wishart, London, 1970).

organize and educate, means which consisted not only in stable parliamentary fractions and in the presence of representatives in local assemblies, but also in newspapers for the dissemination of each party's ideology and machines capable of sustained oral propaganda and organized action.

At the time of writing the Communist Party—and to a lesser extent the Socialist Party—alone answers to that definition.

There are, however, important social strata which no longer look to any political party for the expression of their opinions.

It is an inescapable fact that all those papers which regularly expressed a party ideology have disappeared, excepting only *L'Humanité*, and that the party machines —again with the exception of the Communist Party and, from time to time, the Socialist Party—have dwindled to the status of national caucuses devoid of a solid base save perhaps in election time, caucuses which change, disintegrate and regroup in accordance with the fluctuations of opinion and events.

Thus we see that there is no party outside of the Communist Party having an organized, stable form and able to bring to a class or social stratum the consciousness of itself and its own ends, a party providing in addition an organization for the attainment of those ends.

The major currents and trends which are the somewhat muddled expression of the aspirations of the various classes or social strata today no longer crystallize into the permanent, structured form of major parties. For whether we consider Gaullism, the non-communist Left or the Social Christians, we find that the parties or groups are constantly changing, not just their labels, but their social make-up, their organization and their passwords.

Such political consciousness as there is does not therefore derive from any one party's propaganda or organization, but rather from common information provided by a

Press of which 90 per cent is of neo-capitalist persuasion, or again by radio and television, the media that have done so much to destroy the structure of the parties as they once were. Consequently each person's reactions to the information available to him are governed by the class to which he belongs, so that he will favour, if perhaps somewhat vaguely, either Gaullism or the reformist opposition or else revolution in the abstract.

This factual situation requires a new approach to problems of unity.

4. In such a situation unity cannot be seen as consisting simply in an alliance between parties or political formations, an alliance which may not even be its necessary precondition—except perhaps in the case of the Socialist Party, which still retains some of the characteristics proper to a party in spite of the fact that it succeeds in putting across its own ideology only to a very small proportion of its followers.

In view of the fact that there are today virtually no stable and structured parties to give expression to the consciousness of the social strata, unity must be considered in terms of the direct fusion of those strata. Henceforward the trade union or occupational organizations will play a more important role than that played by the parties in the traditional sense of the term.

It is not only the substance of unity that has changed, but also its aims. To talk of left-wing unity is to go on posing the problem in terms of anti-fascism, terms which were perfectly legitimate in 1936 but had already become less so by 1945 (as, indeed, was pointed out by Maurice Thorez when he raised objections to the very expression of 'left-wing unity', on the grounds that in 1936 this had meant a social regrouping, whereas in 1945 what was involved was national regrouping).

In both cases, however, the aim was clear enough: social

reasons on the one hand and national reasons on the other made it necessary to maintain or re-establish an authentic bourgeois democracy in the face either of a fascist threat or of the fascist occupier's (and his collaborators') transient victory. It was then that the Communist Party coined the apt term of a 'renovated' democracy. In the fight against fascism the restoration or renovation of true political democracy, even though bourgeois and formal, was a valid aim which made it possible to rally round the working class large sections of the middle classes at all levels. National regrouping can even go beyond this, to include opposition to the occupier and his accomplices.

In 1969 the problem must be posed in new terms which are not purely defensive. Aims must be seen as clearly pertaining either to a bourgeois democracy or to a socialist democracy. Now a formal, bourgeois democracy exists in the sense of a democracy that is limited in the political sphere. In a struggle against fascism it is perfectly legitimate to seek to restore, renovate and establish such a democracy on a real footing.

A socialist democracy, on the other hand, is one that permeates the whole of the economy and abolishes patriarchal monarchy in the enterprise.

While intermediary stages between these two kinds of democracy can be postulated, none of those stages can be defined except with reference either to bourgeois democracy or to socialist democracy.

And if we are to define this transitional political form, it must first be considered in relation both to its past, namely formal bourgeois democracy, and to its future, namely concrete socialist democracy.

Concrete socialist democracy is not the antithesis of formal bourgeois democracy; it transcends it, in the Hegelian use of the term, in that it *comprises* all the victories of bourgeois democracy (victories won during several centuries of struggle against feudalism) and frees it of its limitations.

Let us recall the principal of these limitations:

Bourgeois democracy is formal democracy because, as democracy, it is merely political and abstract. It ceases at the factory gates, at the point where the employer's monarchical rule begins and where the 'citizen', theoretically sovereign in the political sphere, once again becomes a 'subject' who is expected to give unconditional obedience to the owner, whether individual or collective, of the means of production.

The struggle for socialism—the struggle, that is, to pass beyond and through bourgeois freedom to a concrete socialist democracy—is a struggle to break out of these limitations and to gain, both within the enterprise and elsewhere, the right to authentic information, the right to culture as well as to training in management, and the right to participation in decision-making.

A corollary of this 'transcendence' is transcendence of the bourgeois concept of 'free enterprise'.

The ideologists of the bourgeoisie extol 'free enterprise' and deplore socialism because the latter 'stereotypes' the work of the producer and destroys the spirit of enterprise. It should be emphasized, however, that socialism in a highly developed country, far from killing the spirit of enterprise, in fact generalizes it, whereas in a capitalist régime it remains the prerogative of the owners of the means of production. This is altogether to the advantage of formal democracy since the proprietors' economic power also confers upon them the privilege of monopoly ownership of the means of communication such as the Press, publishing, the cinema, and so on.

In a bourgeois democracy money, and money alone, reigns supreme, allowing wholesale deception of the masses through the monopoly of the communications media, the corruption of their leaders or representatives and the wilful sabotage of the government by withholding from it the means to implement its policy. Hence political decisions are wholly divorced from the will of the people from which they purport to derive.

That is why all democrats who share a common desire to see democracy expand into socialism should give pride of place in their proposals to the demand for ties between electors, elected, and government, and also, in a more general way, between governors and governed.

The tie between electors and elected can *be effected by means of a binding mandate.* Thus the deputy would not merely be given *carte blanche* on the strength of an abstract programme; rather his election must depend on his providing a precise list of proposed measures together with a time-table for their implementation. The pact between elected and elector would then provide for the latter's dismissal should the time-table not be complied with, as also for the termination of his mandate once the list of proposed measures was exhausted.

The tie between elected and government can be effected by a *contract of legislation* between the government and the majority from which it emanates. As a corollary of the binding mandate this would be a programme whereby the government would be tied to its majority for the duration of the legislature, so that the policy it pursued would not involve a compromise between party caucuses but would emanate directly from the electoral body. A breach of this contract would necessarily involve the dissolution of the representative assembly and a further appeal to the electors. This would obviate the ding-dong action of traditional French politics in which, should a left-wing majority be returned by the electors, it will inevitably be replaced by a ght-wing government at the end of its term of office.

sting tie between governors and governed can be y means of a constant dialogue which would safeguard the rights of the minority and help the govern-ment to keep in touch with the masses. A *permanent dia-logue* on the subject of the programme and the attempt to comply with the time-table laid down for it could be 'institutionalized' through the medium of radio and tele-vision.

Only in this way can political ethics in France be re-stored to health once more.

While it is, of course, true that technological mass media such as computers and television could be exploited to achieve maximum centralization of information and propa-ganda in the service of political power, the same media could also facilitate a maximum dissemination of infor-mation and hence maximum decentralization of decision and initiative.

So great is the potential of technology from this point of view that even 'direct democracy' of an unprecedented kind is now not wholly beyond the bounds of possibility. Rousseau believed that 'the moment a people furnishes itself with representatives, it ceases to be free', and further that 'it is no longer possible for a sovereign to continue exercising his rights among us unless it be in a very small city'.[10] But today, thanks to the computer and to the progress made in methods of disseminating information, we can look forward to a time when there will be a con-stant exchange of information between those at the top and those at the bottom, thus constituting a kind of per-manent plenary assembly of the entire people where, from moment to moment, each individual opinion would be registered, recorded and summarized and where every item of information, having been programmed, would then be made generally available.

This last hypothesis may be no more than a distant dream, but all it represents is an extrapolation and an ulti-mate transition, a transition to a time when the new scien-

10. Rousseau, *Du contrat social*, Vol. III, Ch. 15.

tific and technological revolution, having brought about an unprecedented expansion of the subjective factor, will create the necessary premises and opportunities for every individual's conscious, personal and permanent intervention in the course of history. This is 'the possible' for which we must strive.

For only in this way can we combat the 'alienations' of a State whose relation to the individual is that of an extraneous, unapproachable and hostile reality.

5. The fifth indispensable initiative, an initiative without which none of the others is possible, is *the profound transformation of the very conception of the Party and its organization.*

As we have already recalled, Togliatti hit the nail on the head when, on the morrow of the Twentieth Congress of the Communist Party of the U.S.S.R., he suggested the possibility of 'a new type of Party' which, though still holding to the authentic spirit of Lenin, would diverge from the Party forged by him at a different stage of economic, technological and scientific development and in totally different political circumstances (an underground Party combating the tsarist authorities in different national conditions, i.e. in a country that was predominantly agrarian and backward with a comparatively small working class).

The first essential task today is to consider what form should be assumed by a Communist Party among an educated working class and in a country that is highly developed from the economic and technological point of view; a Party whose hegemony would be exercised on an 'historic bloc' of vast proportions within a nation shaped by two centuries of bourgeois democracy.

During the period immediately following the Twentieth Congress, the Soviet Union—and in its wake the French Communist Party—committed a major error in trying at all costs to save Stalin's 'principles of Leninism', in other words his concept of Party and State. For the French, too, this absence of criticism led to grave consequences, though these were not so immediately maleficent as in countries where the Party was in power and identified itself with the State. Here the replacement of the class by the Party, the Party by the apparatus, and the apparatus by a few leaders, became symptomatic of the survival of Stalinism in the Party organization, a survival which inhibited any real democratization of its internal workings.

Like all other Communist Parties that failed, after the Twentieth Congress, to make any serious critique of Stalinism, contenting themselves with no more than a superficial analysis (hastily cut short) by the Communist Party of the Soviet Union, the French Communist Party persisted in identifying democratic centralism with bureaucratic centralism of a kind which left room only for purely formal democracy.

Marx and Lenin had conceived the organization of the Communist Party in accordance with a dialectical model in which democracy was no more sacrificed to centralism than was the latter to democracy, for without the democracy centralism is bureaucratic and without centralism democracy becomes anarchy.

But because socialism was built initially in countries where the first industrial revolution had only just come into its own, the model it produced bears the stamp, both economic and political, of the early industrial era; in other words it is a mechanistic model.

As such, it derives from Laplacian determinism, according to which the whole universe, the society of the enterprise no less than society in general, is conceived in the image of the machine, just as it is in Leibniz's world of pre-established harmony. The whole is governed at every stage, including manufacture and distribution, by a single law which lays down the only correct mode of action. This form of industrial—as also military—discipline, which had so amply proved its efficacy ever since the industrial revolution of the eighteenth century, inevitably provided the model for the assault period of the revolution, occurring as this did in an industrial society governed by the principles outlined above.

But in a modern complex with automated production such methods of administration and management are now outmoded and constitute an obstacle to development; just as, on the political plane—and for the same reasons—a régime of political power is outmoded.

Hence it would be disastrous for a revolutionary party today to copy those obsolete and cumbrous methods. Rather it should adopt organizational principles in keeping with the new phase in the development of the productive forces.

What fundamental changes have taken place in this respect?

The mechanistic model has been superseded by the cybernetic model.

A feature peculiar to the cybernetic model is its introduction of the feedback factor, that is to say control mechanisms which enable the system to be kept constantly adapted to the new conditions in which it has to function. In the particular case of human society, whether we are concerned with a political party or a factory, this means introducing the subjective factor, in other words the subjectivity of the militants or of the agents of production.

In a centralized and bureaucratic administrative system (the Taylorian and Stalinist methods being typical each of their own kind) society is considered as a mechanism while the individual's initiative, his creative role, is disregarded; the subjectivity of every member of the enterprise, the Party or the nation is suppressed, each individual becoming a link in a chain and every collectivity a 'transmission belt' of impulses emanating from a single centre.

In this era, when the motive force in development is no longer the mechanical accumulation of capital and manpower but rather, and to an increasing extent, the creative development of science and research, the most efficient and also the most 'profitable' method is clearly that which ensures the greatest amount of dynamism in achieving that end. This method of scientific management differs fundamentally from the method practised in earlier, mechanized industry, since it demands that confidence be placed in the spirit of initiative, of responsibility and of creativeness. This applies equally to the organizational and administrative methods of a revolutionary party whose mission it is to promote a policy of *scientific* socialism.

In the highly developed societies of today democratic centralism, if it is to accord with the dialectical inspiration of its founders, Marx and Lenin, must more than ever be conceived in terms of the cybernetic model rather than of the mechanistic model.

This postulates permanent controlling action by the base whose 'feedback' will then enable the decisions reached at the top to be constantly readjusted to the contingencies of the struggle as these arise.

It also postulates that interaction should be not only vertical, between top and bottom and vice versa, but also horizontal, in order to facilitate the cross-fertilization of initiatives and reciprocal intellectual stimulation, not only as between cell and cell, section and section, and federation and federation, but also between the militants at the base and their leaders at the top.

Again it postulates that, within this democratic structure favourable to genuine scientific activity and to constant practical initiative, the managerial role should be revised. This would no longer consist merely in issuing directives and in supervising their proper execution, but first and foremost in eliciting initiatives, in correlating the activities of complex interdependent systems and, finally, in combining those systems into a synthesis and making the most of their autonomous potential.

Clearly this presents a much more complex task than that confronting managers of the old school, but it is the only answer to the demands of the new scientific and technological revolution, as also, and *a fortiori*, to the objectives of a Party which claims to represent scientific socialism.

From this point of view, the militant's daily work—whether in the factory or office, on the farm or at university, and among men and women who do not share his concept of the world or react as he does to events—is for him an invaluable experience. For this reason it is essential that the great majority of leaders, district secretaries or members of the Central Committee should not be permanently appointed officials of the apparatus but should go on doing their ordinary jobs; if they should have to be seconded for Party work, however, this must be on condition that it is for a limited period only and that rotation should be both rapid and compulsory. Besides providing an antidote to bureaucratic tendencies this would facilitate a more 'open' attitude towards the outside as well as a better circulation of ideas.

We are by no means advocating that fractions and organized trends be conceded the right to exist when we suggest that minority opinions within the Party should be made known other than in the truncated and libellous form of the statement refuting them and that the free circulation of ideas should allow an informed majority to express its opinion—a majority, that is, accurately briefed on the various measures put forward as possible solutions to the problems facing the Party. If, as militants, we were pursuing objectives other than those of the Party, it would be absurd to asseverate our allegiance to it. But since our objectives are the same, it ought to be possible to institute open discussions between militants about every fundamental problem and the best means of attaining the desired ends.

For it is thus, and only thus, that we shall be able to rally in a combined effort the millions of Frenchmen who share, with varying degrees of consciousness and resolution, our determination to achieve the construction of socialism.

But we are still very far from having reached that point.

Every time a major problem arises, the rank-and-file militants are kept in ignorance of the various suggestions put forward for its solution. The only information they are given comes after the event in the form of arguments justifying the line adopted by the central leadership.

We need not go far afield to find examples. After the leaders of the Spanish and Italian fraternal Parties at the Moscow Conference had voiced their criticism of and reservations about the attitude of the Soviet leaders towards Czechoslovakia, our Party Press, in its report of this crucial matter failed to provide its readers and the rank-and-file militants with any part of the arguments put forward. Again, on 21 August 1969, exactly one year after the Soviet occupation of Czechoslovakia, when the General Secretary of the Italian Communist Party, Luigi Longo, wrote a leading article for *L'Unità* recalling the principles upon which his Party's opposition had been based, the event was passed over in total silence. From all this it would almost seem as though the rank-and-file militants and the readers of the Party Press were looked upon as minors, incapable of passing judgement and not sensible enough to suggest initiatives regarding problems which might admit of a number of different solutions.

The Party's practice in this respect is neither democratic nor scientific, for both science and democracy demand a free confrontation of methods and hypotheses.

If the French Communist Party is to make its influence felt at home it must declare unequivocally that the socialism it wishes to set up in France is not the kind of socialism imposed upon Czechoslovakia by Brezhnev.

It must also declare that it will engage in a serious and scientific comparative study of the various models of social-ism—Soviet, Chinese, Yugoslavian and Czech (the 'Prague Spring' model)—in order to work out a sound basis for a French model which, while not identifying with any of the others, is able to learn something from each of them.

French communists cannot afford to ignore the under-lying reasons for the Soviet intervention in Czechoslovakia, since to make concessions—either by way of omission or by remaining silent—to the present leaders of Soviet Russia could not fail to compromise the future of socialism in France.

And this for a fundamental reason, namely that the conception of socialism underlying that intervention is one that calls in question the whole political line adopted by the French Communist Party.

There is no ambiguity about the choice confronting us: either we must turn ourselves into the advocates of an extraneous model of socialism such as it would be neither possible nor desirable to set up in this country, or we must strive to achieve independence enough to discover and then establish in France realistic perspectives for a form of socialism adapted to her present economic and social struc-ture.

It must also be clear that the Communist Party cannot, any more than any other party, arrogate to itself, *a priori* and for all time, the title of 'leading Party'.

There can be no doubt, however, that, in principle, the Communist Party is called upon to play an *avant-garde* role:

Firstly, because its mission is to be the consciousness of, as well as the organization for the working class, as also for the 'new historic bloc', a mission in which it will lead all the other forces of the future;

secondly, because Marx's discoveries and Lenin's historical experience can help it to elaborate a scientific conception of social evolution.

But it is still incumbent upon the Party to give practical proof that it is more capable than any other of stimulating initiative in the working class, in the historic bloc and in the mass of the people generally, and also of correlating and concentrating the activities of all the revolutionary forces.

And it is also incumbent upon it to give practical proof of the fact that it regards the teachings of Marx and Lenin as instruments of research and discovery thanks to which it can effectively promote the living science of social evolution.

Where Communist Parties have come to power, they have all too often taken over the role of the working class and, by reducing that class to silence and inaction, have turned Marxism into an instrument of apologetics instead of a means of research. That is why no one will take us at our word.

Daily emulation is the only means of effectively proving superiority. For the only example that will carry any weight will be the example provided by the Party inside the country. The best way of winning over the masses is not to sing the praises while concealing the defects of an alien form of socialism, nor to extol a kind of 'topographical Utopia'; rather something should be done to make the French Communist Party appear, by its internal functioning and also by the perspectives it opens up, as the prototype of socialist democracy.

Then and only then will the Party find its way back to its true function. As Maurice Thorez once said, the Party is not an end in itself but a means towards an end—socialism—which others are capable of realizing in cooperation with it.

Thus the proposition that it is possible to build socialism with a plurality of parties, groups and social organizations, can acquire a concrete meaning for millions of people in France.

To recognize pluralism does not mean regarding the other participants in the construction of socialism merely as 'transmission belts' or as a cloak for the dictatorship of one particular party. Rather, it is to recognize, without reservations, their right and duty to take the initiative in accomplishing the common task.

But an unqualified acceptance of pluralism demands more than this; it demands a dialectical rather than a mechanical relationship between philosophical ideology and political action.

If the Party wishes to be more than a doctrinaire sect, if it wishes to be the leaven for all the forces which, in France, are desirous of building socialism, it cannot afford to have an 'official philosophy', nor can it be in principle either idealist, materialist, religious or atheist.

Needless to say this does not mean repudiating the contribution of Marxist materialism which has facilitated the transition from Utopian to scientific socialism by evolving methods for the study of the objective laws of social life. Rather it means placing that life in its proper context —the context, that is, of scientific research and the revolutionary struggle—instead of in the context of a political dogma whose acceptance is a condition for militant membership and whose rejection would bar all access to leading positions in the Party.

I, who am a materialist, declare that:

If materialism is alone capable of being the basis for efficient scientific research, the proof must be given in conditions of free competition within scientific research itself and nowhere else, least of all in the field of political dogma.

And I, who am an atheist, declare that:

If atheism is alone capable of being the basis for consequential revolutionary action and of conferring on man full responsibility for his history, the proof must be given in conditions of free emulation within revolutionary action itself and nowhere else, least of all in the field of political dogma.

To give a concrete example: in so far as numerous Christians today live their faith in such a way as not to be deterred from possible militant tasks and if, feeling themselves impelled to join the Communist Party, they loyally carry out the tasks this entails, no kind of discrimination can be envisaged. A Christian of this type should have access to any of the leading positions in the Party.

In the course of history too many revolutionary, militant, and combatant movements—such as the Hussite rising in Bohemia and the Peasants' War in Germany—have been conducted under the banner of religion for us to rate a Christian, *a priori*, as a second-class revolutionary.

A pluralist society must necessarily rest on philosophy and politics as distinct entities.

Otherwise dogmatism is inevitable.

Thus the very premises for dialogue have radically changed. Already at an earlier stage in that dialogue the notion of eclectic compromises and of conciliation by way of reciprocal concessions had been superseded. This involved transcending the confrontation of two positions in a synthesis that was not only different but better, a point of view superior to either of the opinions originally in opposition.

The new stage in the dialogue demands as its point of departure, not different opinions about one and the same reality, but rather that reality itself or, more exactly, the problem this poses, a problem for which a common solution is sought.

And the chief problem is to rouse the Party out of its dogmatic slumber which is as disastrous for the Party itself as for the Opposition and for the country as a whole.

That is why the intention of our critique is constructive

rather than polemical and can be summed up as proposing five principal initiatives:

1. To make a fresh analysis of the classes in France as they are now, in the final decades of the twentieth century, in order to define the 'historic bloc' which is the new bearer of the nation's future.

2. To grade claims in accordance with that analysis and to examine the new role likely to be played by the demand for participation in decision-making, in as much as this represents a struggle not only against exploitation but also, and in a more general way, against alienation.

3. To take into account the profound changes that have taken place in the role of the State and of the parties, changes which make it imperative not to mistake parliamentary means for peaceful means in the progress towards socialism.

4. Not to confine the problem of unity to left-wing unity. And, having made that distinction, to elaborate a strategy for a struggle in three main fields, that of the economy, that of politics, and that of culture, a strategy based on the concept of a 'national strike' the possibility of which was presaged by the crisis of May 1968.

5. To transform the Party's methods and style of work by breaking decisively with the Stalinist model, thus posing in new terms the problem of dialectical relations and of cooperation with non-communists, notably by discarding the totalitarian dogmatic conception according to which politics and philosophy form an indissoluble whole; this would entail the acceptance of pluralism, the elaboration of a model of socialism that no longer bears the stamp of Stalinism and, finally, the provision of a prototype for socialist democracy in the very functioning of the Party itself.

# 6 The New Scientific and Technological Revolution and International Relations

Not only does the scientific and technological mutation confront the nations with unprecedented problems; it also upsets the economic and political relations between those nations.

In its spontaneous form, unmodified by human initiative, this change evinces only a negative aspect in that the new scientific and technological revolution develops faster in some countries than in others, thus aggravating existing tensions.

At every stage of this study we have noted that, if the opportunities provided by that revolution are to be fully exploited, there must be not only a considerable concentration of capital in order to set up large automated combines, but also very high labour productivity and a vast market both at home and abroad.

Such is our past heritage, however—our heritage from the period of industrialization and colonialism—that development has been extremely unequal. Moreover, so disparate were the initial handicaps that the new scientific and technological revolution has served only to increase them.

Now the mutation can be accommodated only where certain basic criteria are met, namely the accumulation and concentration of capital, labour productivity, the existence of domestic outlets (a function of the national income *per capita*), and ownership of the basic means of computerization. Hence the world today is split into three strongly differentiated and quite distinct levels.

First there are the countries 'in process of development' which possess none, or virtually none, of the assets we have just mentioned. Strive as these countries may to mobilize their domestic resources, the gulf separating them from the developed countries continues to grow steadily wider.

It is not difficult to discover why this should be. Colonialism from the sixteenth century onwards, like neo-colonialism after the middle of the twentieth, has systematically and to its own profit excluded all possibility of capital accumulation in its subject countries, whether in Asia, Africa or Latin America, so as to preserve a monopoly in industrialization, and to use the countries concerned on the one hand as a source of cheap labour and raw materials, and, on the other, as markets for its capital and for its home industries. This has meant that their national income *per capita* has remained very low and that their standards of living and opportunities for development have been gravely handicapped. World prices for the raw materials they produce have remained fixed at a rate too low to enable them to effect primitive accumulation. The neo-colonial form of industrialization represents more often a mere appendage of the country giving 'aid' than a first material basis for independence and development. As the encyclical, *Populorum progressio*, so rightly points out, the present system ensures that the rich grow richer and the poor poorer.

In those countries whose populations constitute more than two-thirds of that of the under-developed world (i.e. something over a thousand million), the income *per capita* is today less than 100 dollars. Between 1960 and 1967 foreign aid amounting to 1 per cent of the developed countries' national income has permitted an increase of 5 per cent in the national income of the less developed countries. But taking into account an annual population increase of between 2 and 3 per cent, this means that individual purchasing power has risen by something like 2 dollars 50 cents a year—an almost imperceptible rise compared with the rapid growth of national income in the developed countries: West Germany 6.7 per cent, East Germany 9.1 per cent, and the Soviet Union 8.4 per cent.

In Europe in 1952 the gross national product *per capita* was six times higher than that of the under-developed countries. By 1967 it was nine times as high.

The American continent provides an even more striking contrast. Whereas in the United States the gross national product *per capita* exceeds 4000 dollars, in Paraguay it is no more than 100 to 150 dollars, while in Bolivia it is from twenty-five to forty times lower.

This increasing gap is the primary cause of the basic tensions in the world today.

Tension is also growing between the United States and the developed countries generally (whether socialist or capitalist). If we refer again to the criteria enumerated above, it becomes quite evident that as regards the first two—concentration of capital and labour productivity—America is well in the lead. Labour productivity in American industry is more than twice as great as that in the Soviet Union.[1] The gap is striking both in respect of the gross national product *per capita* and of domestic markets: In 1967 the gross national product *per capita* in the United States was 4040 dollars, whereas in Europe the figure varied between 2000 dollars in the wealthier countries such as France, West Germany and Great Britain, and under 1000 dollars in Spain (830), Greece (820), and Portugal (490). Between these two extremes come the socialist countries, the figure for the Soviet Union being 1600 dollars, as compared with 1150 for Japan.

The figures relating to the distribution of computers are no less significant: of the 65,000 computers in use throughout the world in 1968, two-thirds, or 42,000, were

1. Terekhov, 'Economic Competition between Socialism and Capitalism', *La Nouvelle Revue internationale*, Vol. 3, 1968, p. 27.

in the United States, as compared with 13,000 in Western Europe (3800 in West Germany, 2900 in Great Britain, and 2700 in France); the Soviet Union has 4000 and Japan 3400.

Thus the new scientific and technological revolution has considerably aggravated existing inequalities in regard both to opportunity and to the distribution of wealth—so much so, indeed, as to divide the world into three sections between which the gaps, far from diminishing, are growing steadily wider. For even the Soviet Union, which over a long period had developed at a much higher rate than the United States, is now losing ground both in the economic and in the scientific and technological fields, a process which began during the late sixties.

*The fundamental problem confronting us in these final decades of the twentieth century is to narrow the gaps and thus reduce the tensions.*

This is no Utopian project, firstly because we already have the technological potential for its execution, and secondly because the effort required of the developed countries is not just a moral one; indeed it is in their own interests to remedy the situation, since the under-development of one part of the world inevitably fetters and distorts development elsewhere.

If this problem is to be tackled and solved, the first prerequisite is for us to see distortions as they really are and not in the light of our fears and desires, like certain eccentric theorists who, year after year since October 1917, have regularly predicted that socialism will founder in chaos, or again like their opposite numbers who persist in underestimating, not only the contradictions in the socialist system, but also the possibility that capitalism may eventually adapt itself to the development of the productive forces.

Once the Great Powers, and also their allies and satellites, have overcome this first obstacle by ridding themselves of that illusion—the belief, that is, in the apocalyptic self-destruction of their opposite numbers—there will be yet further illusions to combat as regards the underdeveloped countries. Here again there is no room for self-satisfaction. We have already shown in the course of this book that the type of growth in China suggests the possibility of more than one criterion of development. The Western (and this includes the socialist) countries will have to do more than rid themselves of the colonialist illusion that they are the only centres of initiative and that it is from them alone that all values emanate. The use made by the Chinese to effect primitive accumulation by means other than those employed by European capitalism in the early nineteenth century or by Soviet socialism at the beginning of the twentieth, conjures up unprecedented possibilities for countries where the population is increasing far more rapidly than in the West and where different conceptions of man and of the world may lead to equally unprecedented ways of exploiting those possibilities. The dialogue between civilizations has only just begun.

Only if the dialogue is genuine—a confrontation, that is, in which each is convinced from the start that there is something to be learnt from the other—will it be possible to reduce tensions, and this in turn can only be achieved by bridging the gaps and by working towards that integration of the world upon which, at the present stage of technological development, its survival depends.

Every day brings new objective possibilities that could enable us to resolve those tensions and bridge those gaps: the discovery of new sources of energy (by the end of this century nuclear energy may well be only one kind among several), new sources of foodstuffs through the exploitation of marine flora and marine chemistry, as in the synthesis of chlorophyll and of proteins, or again, new possibilities for the distribution and conveyance of energy, produce and information. Modest though this prospectus may be, it nevertheless provides an assurance that even if, as has been predicted, the world population has grown to more than five thousand million by the year 2000, technological solutions could be found in the near future, not only to the problems of food supplies but also to those of primary economic resources in all countries throughout the world.

*This solution postulates the renunciation of bloc politics which are a survival of the past, of the industrial era.* It is true that, so long as countries possessed only conventional weapons, the acquisition of more infantry divisions, guns, tanks or aircraft played a not inconsiderable role by providing a quantitative superiority that could be decisive. In the age of missiles and the H-bomb, bloc politics are outmoded even from a military point of view.

The capitalist world must be held primarily responsible for the creation of blocs. For in the hope of 'rolling back' and containing communism, and in response to the plea made by Churchill to Senator Fulton of the U.S.A., that world organized itself militarily into an 'Atlantic Pact' under American leadership, so carrying the class struggle on to the international plane. This aggressive coalition led inevitably to its corollary, the Warsaw Pact.

The blocs were constituted both on a class basis and on an ideological basis. Now history has shown that every action undertaken within these blocs has run counter to the ends that were supposedly being sought. America has presented herself to the world as the champion of liberty, yet her interventions in Guatemala, in the Dominican Republic and in Vietnam, not to mention her more clandestine ventures in the Congo, Greece and throughout Latin America, have all basically resulted in the victory of the most reactionary—not to say fascist—forces, a victory which has cost the people their freedom.

Though the opposite bloc, that of the Warsaw Pact, has played a role that is infinitely less harmful, its interventions have invariably been motivated by the desire to impose on its weaker partners the authoritarian socialist model of Russian provenance. This policy has had momentous consequences. On the economic plane the systematic overvaluation of the currency of the Comecon (socialist Common Market) countries has proved a major obstacle to relations, whether commercial or otherwise, with the rest of the world.

The military, economic and ideological absurdity of bloc politics is becoming ever more apparent.

Where the United States is concerned the experience of Vietnam is crucial. The most powerful military machine of all time is being held in check by a small nation welded together by its struggle for independence and enjoying the material support of China and the U.S.S.R. America's economy has been profoundly distorted by this war, which has also led to the collapse of her prestige throughout the world.

It is an established fact that, because of her imperialistic and neo-colonial policies, the United States is utilizing only the by-products of her true potential, what might be termed the military and economic 'offal' of her true superiority. For where she excels is in the fields of science and technology.

Today the United States can no longer withdraw into her own continent in the name of some new version of the Monroe Doctrine.

Hers is a world-wide vocation—but not, as Burnham thought, to impose her military hegemony, nor to restore an economic colonialism whose bankruptcy is everywhere apparent, nor yet to claim the leadership of an ideological crusade, being, as she is, wholly devoid of any ideology and quite incapable of assigning herself human goals.

For her the solution is not 'disengagement' but a radically new kind of engagement based on the dissemination of knowledge, with no political strings attached, the scientific and technological knowledge of which economic wealth and military potential are no more than by-products.

Only in this way can the United States achieve one hundred per cent efficiency in her immense productive machine and create the preconditions for an economic boom unprecedented in her history.

As for the Soviet Union, perseverance in a repressive system at home and within the bloc under its sway and also failure to create political conditions capable of assuring the success of the economic reform would inexorably fetter the country's development, would widen still further the gap between itself and the United States, and postpone, if not indefinitely at least for a very long time, all chance of effecting the full realization of socialism and the transition to communism. The consequences of intervention in Czechoslovakia have shown just how damaging such a policy can be: It has sapped the military strength of the member countries of the Warsaw Pact, has brought about economic stagnation in Czechoslovakia, once the most advanced country of the group, has caused an ideological split in the socialist camp, and has diminished the influence of socialism throughout the whole of Europe.

It is significant, too, that bloc politics have everywhere suffered repeated reverses. The disintegration of the imperialist world under the assault of national liberation movements, the break-up of S.E.A.T.O. in Asia and of N.A.T.O. in Europe after the withdrawal of France, and the dissensions by which 'Europe' is now torn, have all dealt telling blows to American hegemonic pretensions in the capitalist world.

In the socialist camp and within the group formed under the Warsaw Pact in response to the threats of the Atlantic Treaty, the shocks have been no less violent. The most spectacular was the invasion of Czechoslovakia and its consequences, but other deep fissures have also formed: Since the initial schism in the socialist world, born of Yugoslavia's excommunication in 1948, there has been the Sino-Soviet split whereby the contradictions have assumed universal dimensions, followed by the development of centrifugal forces initiated by Romania within the economic community of socialist countries (Comecon).

This irreversible trend towards the dislocation of the blocs affords proof that these methods cannot resolve the international problems of today, which is to say that they cannot reduce the tensions engendered by the existence of three separate levels of development.

Integration cannot be brought about either by methods involving the mechanical, hierarchical subordination of the weak to the strong or by the accretion of the combined forces of a number of satellites to a major power.

Nor can integration be effected by means of a 'peaceful co-existence' whose sole basis is economic competition in which the object of the less fortunate is to 'catch up and surpass' the rival who is in the lead.

Hence to propose, as did Stalin, Khrushchev and Brezhnev successively, that Russia's aim should be to 'catch up with and overtake' the United States would be to steer her into an impasse, for the true vocation of a socialist country is not simply quantitative emulation of advanced capitalist countries, but *the creation of a new model of civilization* which would offer a real alternative to a capitalist system dominated by the blind law of growth for growth's sake and incapable of setting itself ends that are truly human.

In the same way, though in a wholly different context, it would be wrong to suggest, with Servan-Schreiber, that in order to safeguard her independence, Europe should ape the actions of the United States, a policy that could only increase her tutelage *vis-à-vis* the latter.

*The central problem* is to conceive and to bring to fruition entirely novel forms of integration which alone will permit *the historic bridging of the gap* separating the industrialized from the under-developed countries and the United States from Europe.

The decisive initiative for every country will consist in taking stock in order to discover what its own contribution could be: in the case of the United States, not force of arms (which has led to such resounding defeats), nor economic colonization (which has inflamed anti-American sentiment throughout whole continents, from Asia to Latin America), but rather the incontestable power of expansion of her scientific and technological potential. In the case of the Soviet Union, not dogmatic and unwavering adherence to the myth of a unique and perfect model for the construction of socialism, but rather an indispensable and harrowing reappraisal that will enable her to restore the prestige of the October Revolution as the only real alternative to the capitalist régime, and to revitalize the influence of socialism as the only system capable of safeguarding the autonomy of man in the era of the new scientific and technological revolution and of putting forward truly human goals for the latter's development.

Where China is concerned, it would be a disaster were she to isolate herself by dogmatization and by the extrapolation of her own model on to the rest of the world instead of using her own experience to help other countries and other socialist parties towards a better understanding of the need for a diversity of socialist models and for developmental criteria; towards a better understanding, too, of the need for objectivity in regard to values and to the types of civilization and socialism that have evolved in the Western world.

Much more could be said about the initiatives to be taken by each country, but what really needs stressing is the fact that all this is not just pious exhortation. In each of the countries we have cited (though in the case of China information is now rather scarce) there are men who have already become aware of these problems, among them more especially those who, as scientists, play a leading role in the creation of their country's technological potential and know what course should be pursued if their work is to be fully effective. In America today there are many nuclear research workers, economists, sociologists, students, academics and militants who would like to see a revival of the trade union movement such as would rally forces capable of holding their own against the military-industrial complex. In the Soviet Union there are eminent physicists, great writers and innumerable militants, all of whom are aware of the malpractices perpetrated by the bureaucratic-military complex.

In other countries, such as France and Italy, where the opposition has a less arduous task, there are numerous regenerative forces to combat hierarchical sclerosis. Once they have won the struggle for secession from a bloc, those forces can insist upon non-alignment.

Thus the class struggle is assuming a new shape at international level.

The generation now coming into the world is starting life at a time when the new scientific and technological revolution is creating for it conditions of thought, work and existence radically different from those of preceding generations.

Will these forces be able to combine, beyond all divergencies, so as to carry forward the class struggle of the new historic bloc, setting an example of integration in diversity and of an international division of labour which could turn the twenty-first century into the era of permanent revolution where living conditions and human prospects are concerned?

At international level the great initiative is that which will make possible mutual consultation and the exchange of information.

The aim here is to rid ourselves, in the field of international relations, of intercourse determined by competition, rivalry and jungle confrontations engendered by the class struggle at international level and to put in its stead relations that correspond to the demands and possibilities of the new scientific and technological revolution. Relations which correspond, in other words, to a new, unprecedented form of socialism whose creation demands new, historical initiatives both on the theoretical and on the practical plane.

For the working class and the new historic bloc the problem whose solution is the precondition for the solution of all the rest is the problem posed by *the growing inequality in levels of development and the tensions to which this situation gives rise*.

Until that basic problem has been tackled it will be worse than useless to pin our faith on some miraculous form of negotiation capable of ensuring peace and a safe future without in any way changing objective relations as they now are.

For in this field the dominant idea has hitherto been that of hegemony, which has been the aim of the more powerful and the aspiration of the weak. Both have thought in terms of blocs or opposing camps, either as a stage on the road to hegemony or as a means of resisting it and, perhaps, of catching up with the strong.

On such a basis all those vital negotiations upon which the life or death of a civilization depend, are doomed to failure or to impotence. And this is so whether the negotiations are concerned with major problems such as nuclear disarmament or aid to under-developed countries, or again with questions raised in the UN, of which the most typical as also the most topical example is that of the Middle East. Indeed, in the final analysis this latter instance poses the problem of the relations between development and under-development, a problem whose terms are rendered all the more complex not only by the fact that the circumstances derive from the time of colonialism when the Great Powers settled everything behind the backs of the colonial countries, but also by the fact that, in the present confrontation, all the blocs are involved. This means that, even if agreement is reached—at least on paper—the international community has no powers to enforce it in practice.

For underlying the abstract agreements are the real relations between levels of development (and between the blocs they engender) and these relations impose their concrete logic in the form of impediments.

This is the state of affairs seen in global terms.

It is true that outside the blocs a policy of non-alignment is taking shape (though for many participants non-alignment is a programme or a hope rather than actual fact). This policy proposes to attenuate the contradictions produced by bloc politics in international relations, to ban the use of force, to safeguard the right of all peoples to equality and self-determination, and to promote cooperation between countries, regardless of régime.

Since the Afro-Asian Conference proclaimed its principles at Bandung in April 1955 these objectives, which are also those of the United Nations Charter, have been reaffirmed by the fifteenth session of the United Nations General Assembly, and also by the non-aligned countries at their conferences in Belgrade in 1961, in Cairo in 1962 and 1964, and in New Delhi in 1966, and, finally, by the first World Conference on trade and development convened in Geneva in 1964 by the United Nations.

It was undoubtedly the non-aligned countries and, under their pressure, the United Nations Organization, which first gave expression to the objectives most conducive to improved relations between the peoples. Concrete measures have been proposed: the reassessment in the world market of the prices of raw materials exported by the under-developed countries, new forms of the international division of labour and, finally, the organization of aid by international bodies in such a way as to obviate bilateral relations (tainted as these invariably are with neo-colonialism), and also to obviate the hegemony within those international bodies of the most powerful contributor. There were also some remarkable proposals for the transfer of investment from armaments to the development of the less wealthy nations' economic resources.

All these practical projects were, and still remain, perfectly valid and, were they to be applied, there can be no doubt that they would be efficacious.

But the problem is how to apply them. For so long as these great disparities in development continue to survive along with the ideologies and tensions they engender in each camp and every country, so long will those who—as in the Third World—have reason and numbers on their side still not be strong enough to exploit these advantages.

Each camp experiences like a recoil the maleficent effect of the ideology it has framed to justify the blind workings of its policy and economy. In the course of this study we have attempted to pose this problem in respect of every major country and every major political orientation.

We have tried successively to show how anti-communist ideology is used in the United States to justify the arms race, the Vietnam war and support for the most retrogressive dictatorships in many parts of the world. At the same time that ideology cloaks a deep-seated distortion of the American economy: a hegemonic policy which still inspires American practice even if it is no longer cynically and explicitly stated as in 1948, in Burnham's time; a form of repression no longer as extreme as erstwhile McCarthyism but liable at any moment to flare up again; an inability to solve the problem of colour or of poverty, or to meet the challenge of youth; a blind and deformed growth wholly devoid of human ends which squanders its opportunities by a very inadequate use, not only of its productive potential, but also of the possibilities made available by research and creativity.

We have shown how, in the Soviet Union, the state of siege and the feverish anxiety it engendered—which persisted even after encirclement from the outside had been relaxed—combined with the necessity (later to become an obsession) of 'catching up and surpassing', induced symmetrical distortions in the country's economy. These were due largely to the nuclear and space race (even more onerous for Russia than for the United States with her far higher national income), to a nervous ideological retreat for fear of 'ideological subversion' and, lastly, to the ensuing retardation of the development of the superstructures, with an anti-scientific and anti-democratic conception of State and Party. The consequence of this has been to inhibit the implementation of the economic reform and to fetter the new scientific and technological revolution which alone can make possible the full realization of socialism and the transition to communism.

Much the same thing applies to China and to a number of other countries.

For certain roads are blind alleys. The endeavour, for instance, to achieve hegemony under pretext of pushing back or containing communism everywhere in the world. Or the endeavour to 'catch up and surpass' in a spirit of rivalry which encourages the ultimate illusion that even America is susceptible of bolshevization.

Or again, the endeavour to surmount under-development by following in the footsteps of the developed countries and by aping their methods. It is an established fact that under-development cannot be surmounted by capitalist means; no country in the Third World has been able either to gain true independence or perceptibly to raise its economic potential and standard of living in this way. Those countries in Latin America, Africa and Asia which remain part of the capitalist world are still under-developed and will continue to be so.

Of all the under-developed countries only China, Vietnam and Cuba have succeeded in 'taking off' and this for the very reason that they have radically transformed social relations and have undertaken the construction of socialism in accordance with specific models that are not the same as the European models.

Although the term 'socialist' has been besmirched by countries which rely on *dirigiste* formulas while compounding quite happily with neo-colonialist laws, elsewhere practical attempts have been made to escape from this state of illusion and bondage. This has happened in a number of countries, but more notably in the United Arab Republic, in Syria, in Algeria (especially in Ben Bella's time), in Mali—before the putsch inspired by neo-colonialism plunged the country back into chaos—and, finally, in Guinea, where, however, dangerous attempts have been and are being made to reverse the trend, attempts which threaten at any moment to jeopardize the whole experiment.

Precisely because the new scientific and technological revolution opens up such magnificent prospects—prospects which have nothing in common with what we, in this chaotic world, have known before—class problems are assuming vast and agonizing proportions. The old automatisms, functioning blindly under the compulsion of inertia, exacerbate existing inequalities and tensions.

At this level initiative cannot be confined to the formulation of a programme; it must involve a change of method, thus achieving the necessary inversion.

There are programmes enough, as we have seen, and excellent measures have been advocated.

The change in method consists in paying more attention to *conditions of realization.*

Since the difficulties arise *at the level of each country concerned, it is there, and there alone, that the necessary provisions can be made,* and there that action must be taken.

This cannot be done by an international body alone where, as we have seen, neither weight of numbers nor force of reason will necessarily prevail.

What must be done in each country is to encourage an awareness of the new problems posed by the scientific and technological revolution, to mobilize public opinion and, more important still, to mobilize the working class and the new historic bloc by inducing awareness of these problems and by providing objective information about similar attempts that are being made in other countries.

If such mobilization is to be effective it must, from the very start, activate the most dynamic elements of the new 'historic bloc', which is itself a product of the great mutation.

The originality of this trend consists in the attempt to effect world unity and the unity of man, not by way of hegemony, of negative toleration or an imposed uniformity, but by way of integration. From that integration there would arise a complex form of unity in which each nation and each régime would develop in accordance with its own particular law. It is wholly unrealistic to expect that peace will result from a renunciation of socialism by the U.S.S.R. or from the overthrow of capitalism in the United States, for we have at most ten years in which to halt our headlong progress towards the apocalypse of famine and total destruction.

*What can be done here and now is to press, in the United States, for a form of capitalism that has human goals; in the Soviet Union for the democratization of socialism and, in the Third World, for the discovery of new criteria and new methods of development.*

If they are to be effective, the means must not gainsay

the ends in view: hence no world parliament, still less a world executive.

Concerted discussion is necessary to keep abreast of incipient problems in all their aspects and possible consequences. *Thus the first stage can only be the initiation of a true dialogue between civilizations*—those of the East, of the West, and of the South.

The international organization that will form the context for the dialogue and discussion cannot have as its objective the formulation of theses of an imperative or directive nature. Rather it will seek to provide themes for research and deliberation.

The organization should not be made up of official 'delegates' from states, parties or professional or cultural organizations. Though it should not exclude anyone merely because of his membership of, or even his leading role in, a particular institution, any intervention on his part arising directly out of that role must be precluded. His contribution would be assessed, not in terms of his function, but of the help it affords in the posing and solution of problems, or of the value of the information supplied.

Concerted discussion would gain substance from the fact that it would not take place in formal sessions at regular intervals but rather in relation to a particular problem. These occasions would facilitate the free flow of ideas and the elaboration of provisional syntheses whose dissemination and popularization would activate the consciousness of millions of men and women.

Hence it will be essential to have a permanent organ of expression, an international review whose aim is not polemical but exploratory. This would provide a constant overall view of changes as they occur and of their effect upon each other as also of the initiatives that become possible and necessary as human relations alter, thus permitting, on the one hand the full deployment of the new scientific and technological revolution with all its implications and, on the other, the creation by that revolution, not of new alienations but of conditions permitting each and every man to attain his fullest development.

The first and chief protagonists in this combined effort comprising information, synthesis and exploration are today those in whom the decisive power to metamorphose the world is vested, the scientists and research workers.

No doubt an easy target for sarcasm is provided by what some might derisively call the 'eggheads' and technocrats' International'. Yet the very nature of the enterprise should exclude any such analogy, if only because its whole tendency is against the issuing of either directives or advice. Its only aim and object is to respond to the need for *an organized consciousness of change.* Hence there is no question of its replacing either states, parties, churches, trade unions, or major international institutions such as the UN or UNESCO.

In the age of the new scientific and technological revolution, the way to socialism in the developed countries can no longer be governed by the principle evolved for times and countries that were predominantly agrarian, namely that of the alliance of workers and peasants. In forming the new 'historic bloc', the primary task—and one that will determine the future—*is the union of the forces of labour and of culture.*

The construction of new historic blocs presents a rather different aspect in the developing countries because of the latters' class structure. We do not claim to possess the key to this problem (any more than we claim to have all the answers to the questions raised in this book), but if it is to be explored at all the development of these countries should not be seen as a duplication of the course taken by the 'Western' countries during the nineteenth and twentieth centuries. As the Chinese Revolution has shown, it is possible to proceed directly from an agrarian-feudal society to socialism without any intermediate capitalist phase. Hence it would seem probable that economic and technical backwardness could be overcome, not by industrialization of the old type, but by a less indirect approach to the new scientific and technological revolution. The question of the diversity of developmental criteria arises at all levels. In the developing countries, it is not a case of substituting, either in international relations or in individual nations, a theory of unequal development for the Marxist concept of contradiction and the class struggle, nor is it a case of juxtaposing these, but rather of bringing them into relation and demonstrating the extent to which, in the age of the new scientific and technological revolution, unequal development demands new forms of struggle for the working class and the new historic bloc.

This is not to consider technology within a technological context, but in the wider perspective of the class struggle which alone can assign to it its highest goal—a goal whose first inception must be credited to Marx—man's liberation from labour and his disalienation.

The essential task, as we have tried to show all through this book, is to help the new 'historic bloc' to consolidate and to become conscious of its unity, for that bloc and it alone can open up future perspectives, originate decisive historical initiatives and rally forces capable of effecting the change.

The ideas put forward in this final chapter are no more than suggestions for a more detailed analysis of the new circumstances governing the class struggle at international level, in an age when the new scientific and technological revolution calls in every country for the initiative that will engender an awareness of the new historic bloc whose construction has now become possible.

It is not, therefore, a Utopian proposal to create an 'authority' that would transcend the classes and the blocs which, at international level, express the class struggle.

The intention is rather the world-wide organization of

the concerted forces in whose hands lies the future of mankind and the future of every nation: the working class, and the new historic bloc to which each country is giving birth.

The accomplishment of this historical task was entrusted by Marx and Lenin—and rightly so—to the Communist Parties.

In so far as the initiative we propose has become necessary, it is only to make good the lapses of those to whom the task was entrusted, lapses resulting from the theoretical bankruptcy of the Soviet leaders whose main preoccupation is to impose on others their outdated model of socialism, a preoccupation that finds its echo in the Chinese camp.

The two greatest powers in the socialist world, the Soviet Union and China, are today led by men who in effect seek to impose on other Communist Parties their own exclusive model of socialism (whatever circumlocutions they may use to mask their intentions). This has led not only to the tragic confrontation of these two powers and to a split in the movement, but also to a world-wide loss of influence for socialism and to the weakening of those individual Communist Parties which submit to the ideological influence of either of these two dogmatisms.

Such are the circumstances that have brought socialism to the verge of its great turning-point.

This is not to say that existing workers' parties should be supplanted, still less combated; rather they should be helped to accomplish the mutation that will enable them, in all countries, to assert their hegemony within the new historic bloc.

If the leading organs of the workers' parties should prove impervious to the need to discover a new type of relation permitting common theoretical deliberation, the manual and non-manual workers, who are the motive element in the new historic bloc and to whom the demand for this new form of theoretical deliberation is a lived experience, would find ways of bringing about that deliberation and would thus restore vitality to the movement by paving the way for the regeneration of its leading organs.

The accomplishment of this task demands criticism of a new kind—a kind that is positive as well as negative. For the discovery of the contradictions inherent in a system is not enough to demonstrate the *impossibility* of accepting the existing order or disorder. It is also and above all necessary to demonstrate the *possibility* of conceiving and realizing a different order, of *changing the rules of the game* so as to reduce the gap between what, henceforward, is in fact realizable and what is actually and pitifully real.

This inversion of the critical method is a result of the great mutation and provides unmistakable evidence of what can be achieved; far from leading to the construction of a Utopia, it demonstrates, as Gorz once said, the need for change by the very fact of its possibility.

This is not to suggest that a ready-made doctrine should be brought 'from the outside' to the working class and the historic bloc as a whole. Rather it means, as Marx has indicated, becoming conscious of the intrinsic demands of that class and of that bloc and inducing in them a clear sense of their implicit goal in accordance with what is actually possible. To do so postulates, firstly, uninterrupted attention to and interrogation of spontaneous consciousness by means of a 'working-class inquiry' as broadly outlined by Marx in 1880 and, secondly, a scientific consideration of the current mutation and the prospects it offers.

The initiative we are suggesting at international level is nothing less than the global coordination of those national initiatives and also of that perception of the possible which alone will permit recognition of the need to change the rules of the game and to eradicate all belief in miracle-working negotiations capable of settling difficulties without getting to their objective core. Only in this way can we tackle the real problem upon whose solution that of all the rest depends: the problem of eliminating the disparate levels of development from which all tensions derive.

In this world and in every country in the world there are forces capable of solving the problem that is the matrix of all the rest.

Our first task must be to gain a clear idea of the objectives, the long-term proposals and the methods best suited to their aspirations and to their intrinsic demands, which are, indeed, their implicit philosophy. 'Ideas,' Marx wrote, 'become a material force once they have gripped the masses.' And it is that force we must encourage to develop and grow. Our task is further to be the catalyst of the great mutation, the living element in the thought of the individual, by providing all these real forces at all times with information, syntheses and forecasts.

As the leaven in the great human ferment taking place during these final decades of the twentieth century, this enterprise must help to initiate the dialogue of those who love the future.

It is no longer possible to remain silent.


*Paris, October 1969.*

Roger Garaudy

Roger Garaudy is a Professor at the University of Poitiers. He is a Docteur ès Lettres of the Sorbonne, and holds a doctorate in science from the Soviet Academy of Science. Until his expulsion from the Central Committee and later from the Party itself, he was a member of the Politburo of the French Communist Party and Director of the Centre for Marxist Studies and Research. His published works include studies of Marxist humanism and ethics, Marxism and Existentialism, and the problem of freedom in the twentieth century.